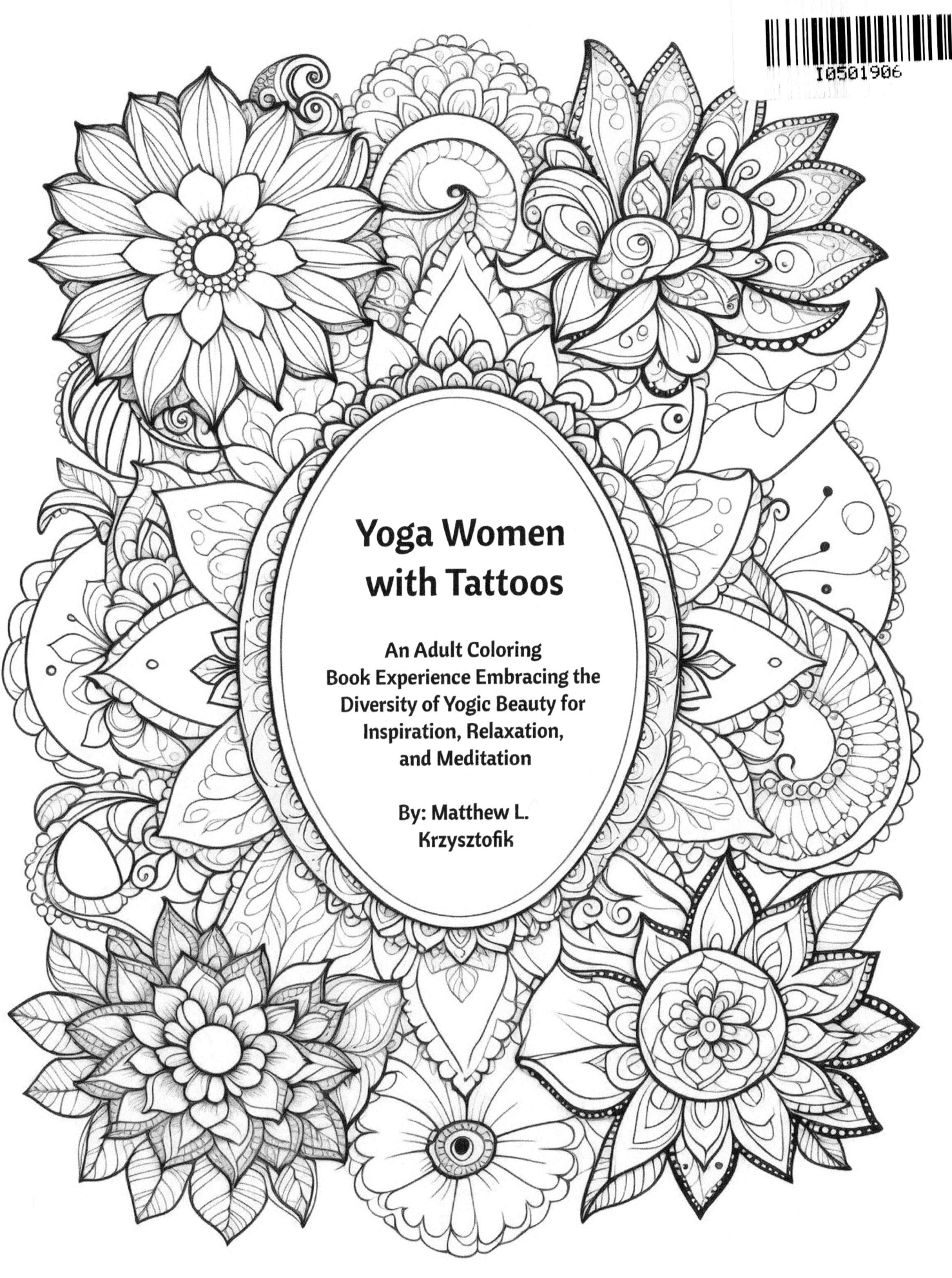

Yoga Women with Tattoos

An Adult Coloring Book Experience Embracing the Diversity of Yogic Beauty for Inspiration, Relaxation, and Meditation

By: Matthew L. Krzysztofik

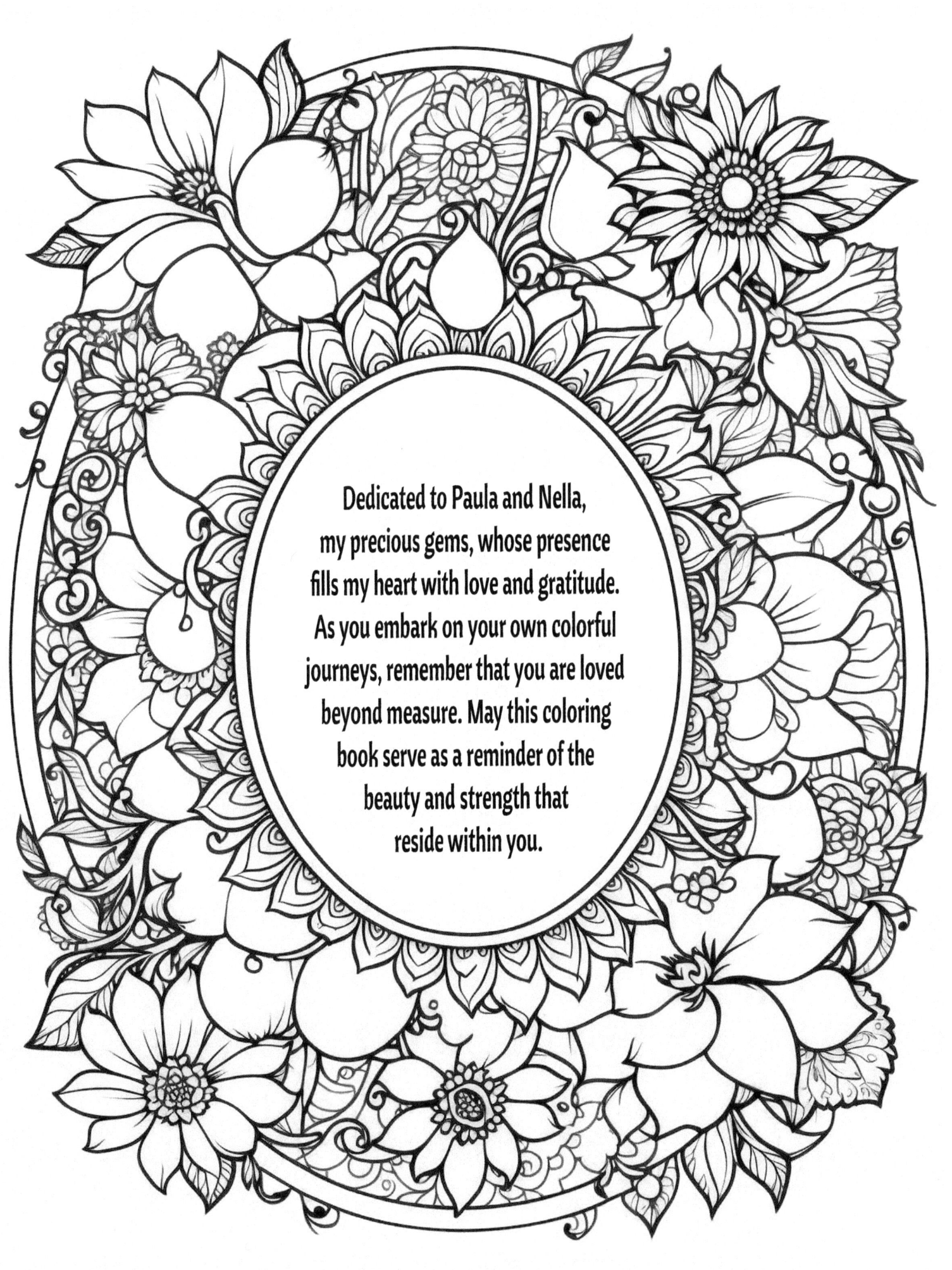

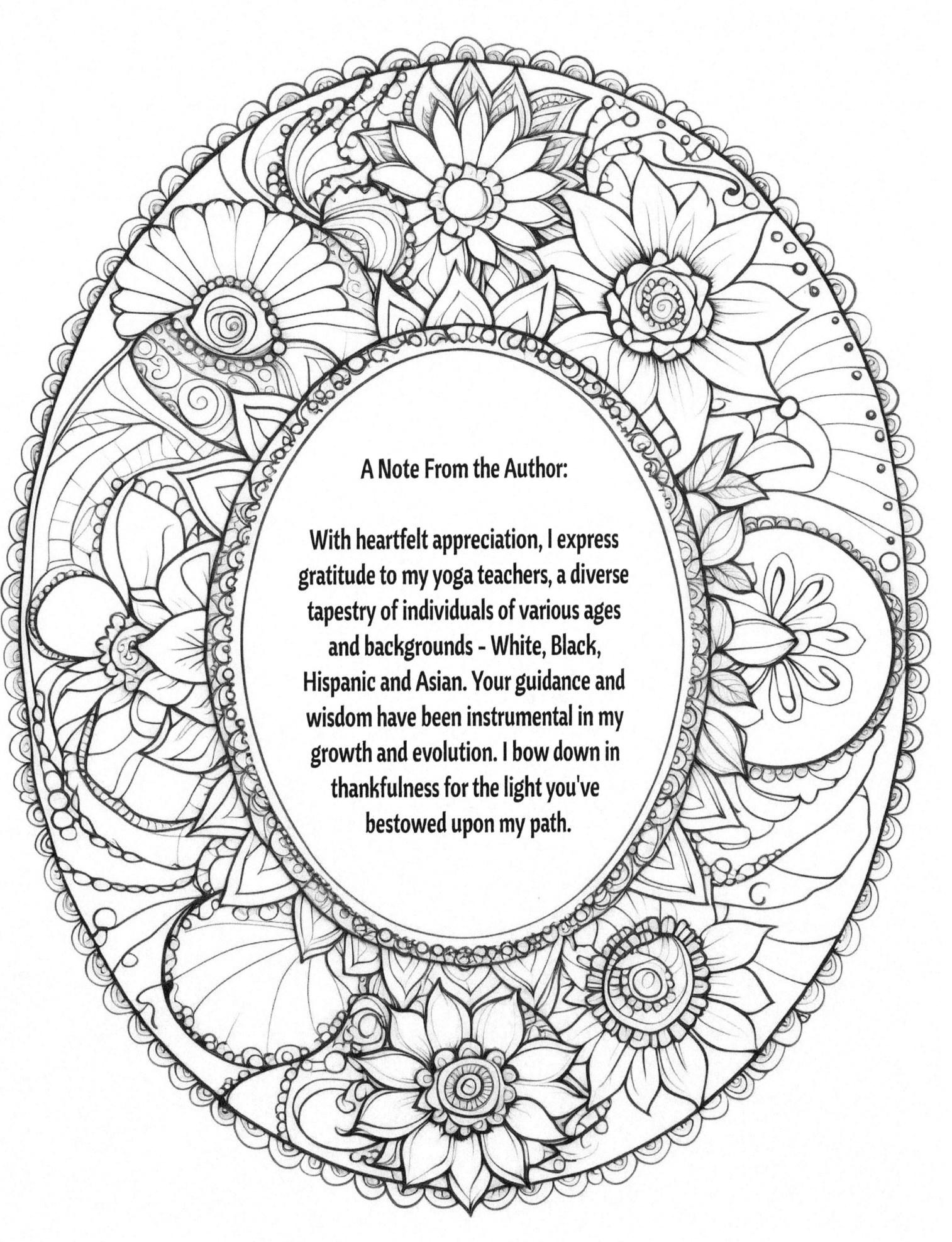

A Note From the Author:

With heartfelt appreciation, I express gratitude to my yoga teachers, a diverse tapestry of individuals of various ages and backgrounds - White, Black, Hispanic and Asian. Your guidance and wisdom have been instrumental in my growth and evolution. I bow down in thankfulness for the light you've bestowed upon my path.

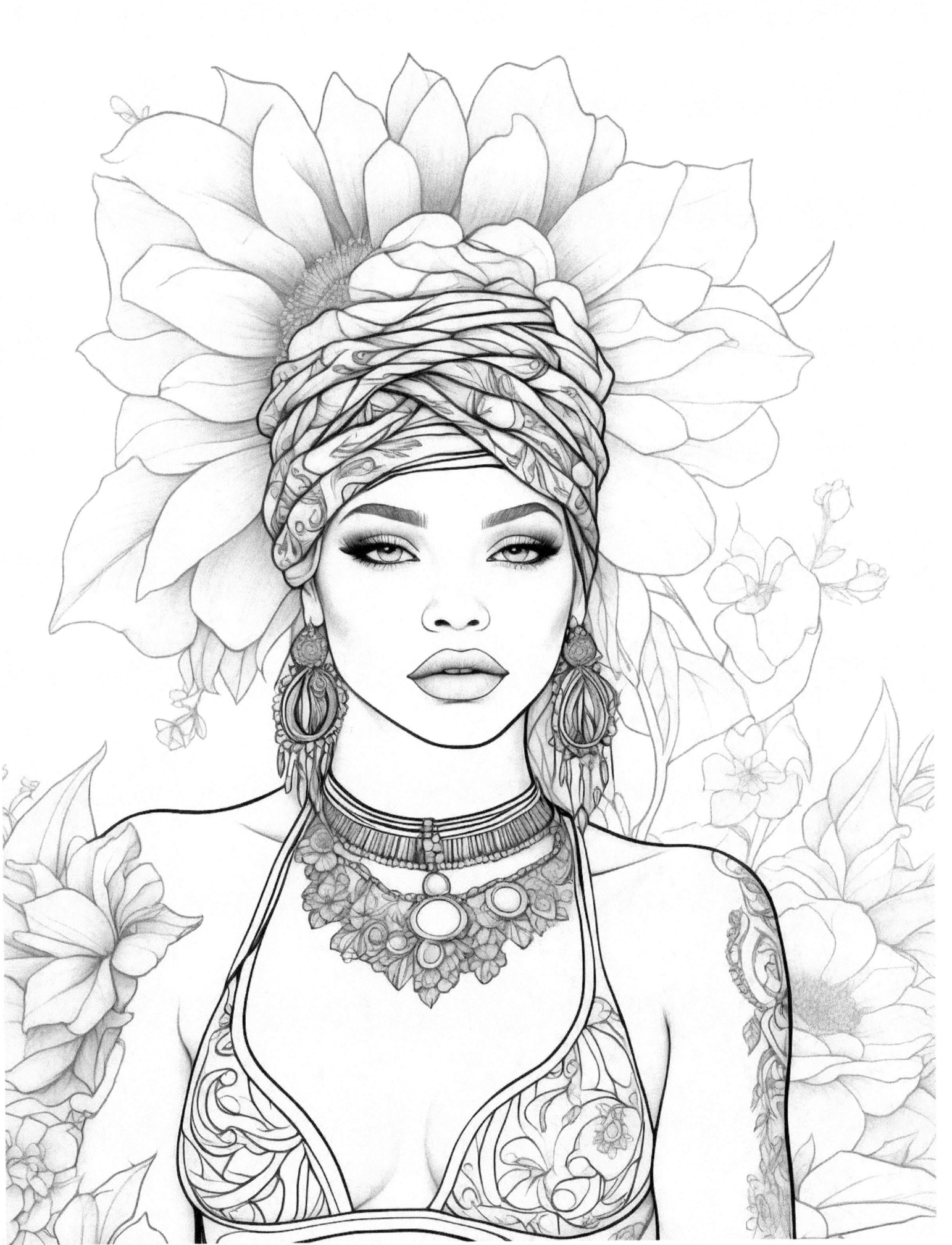

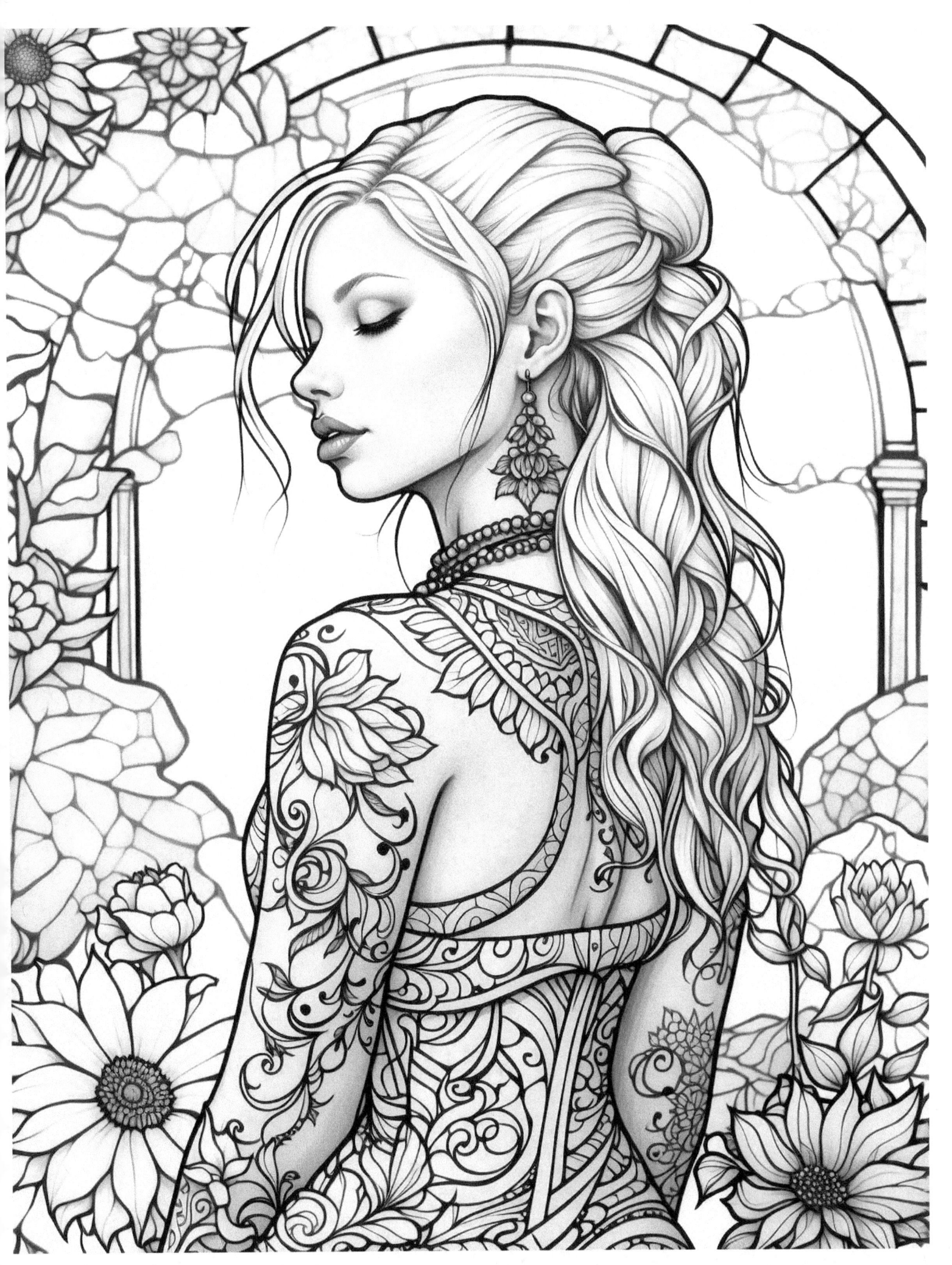

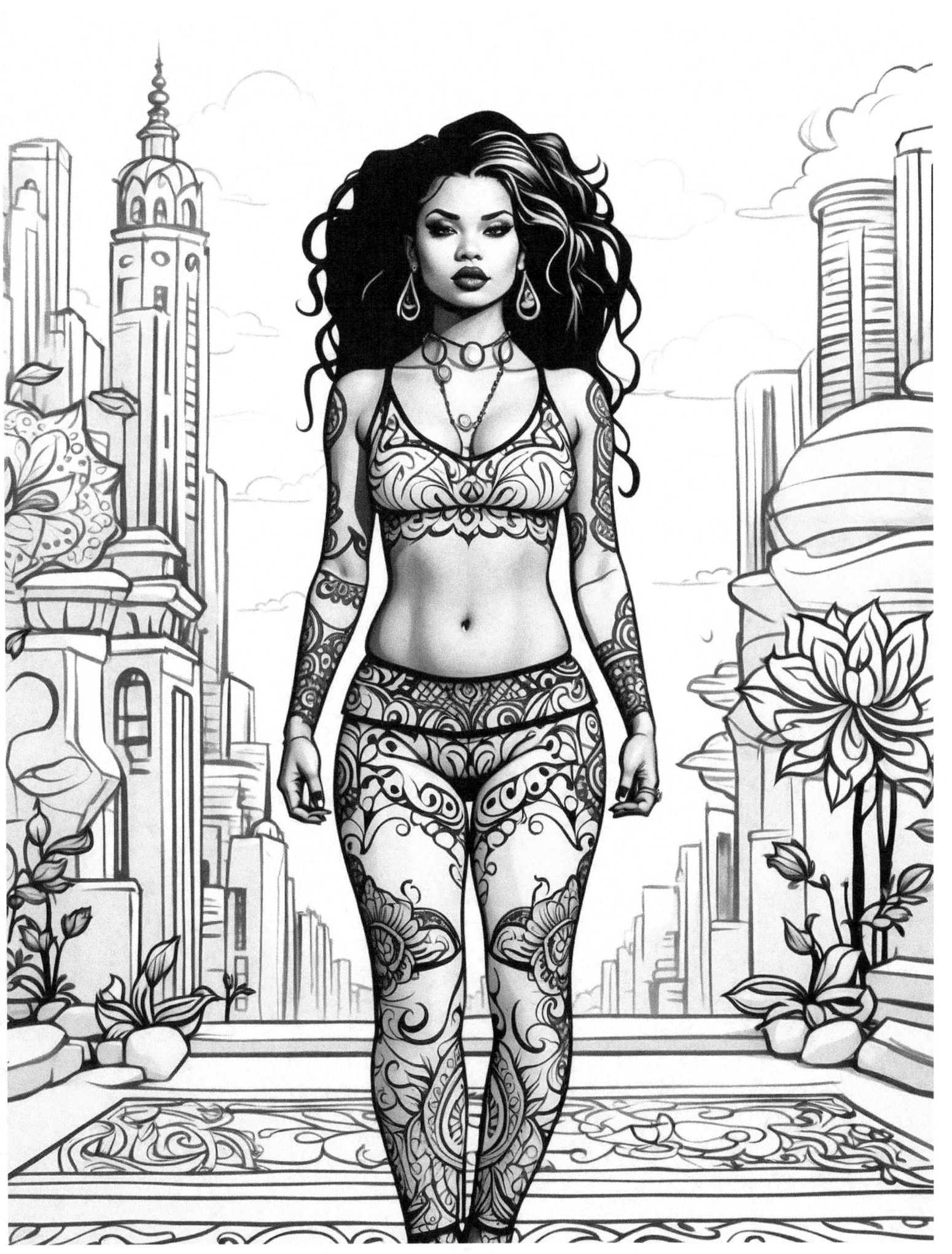

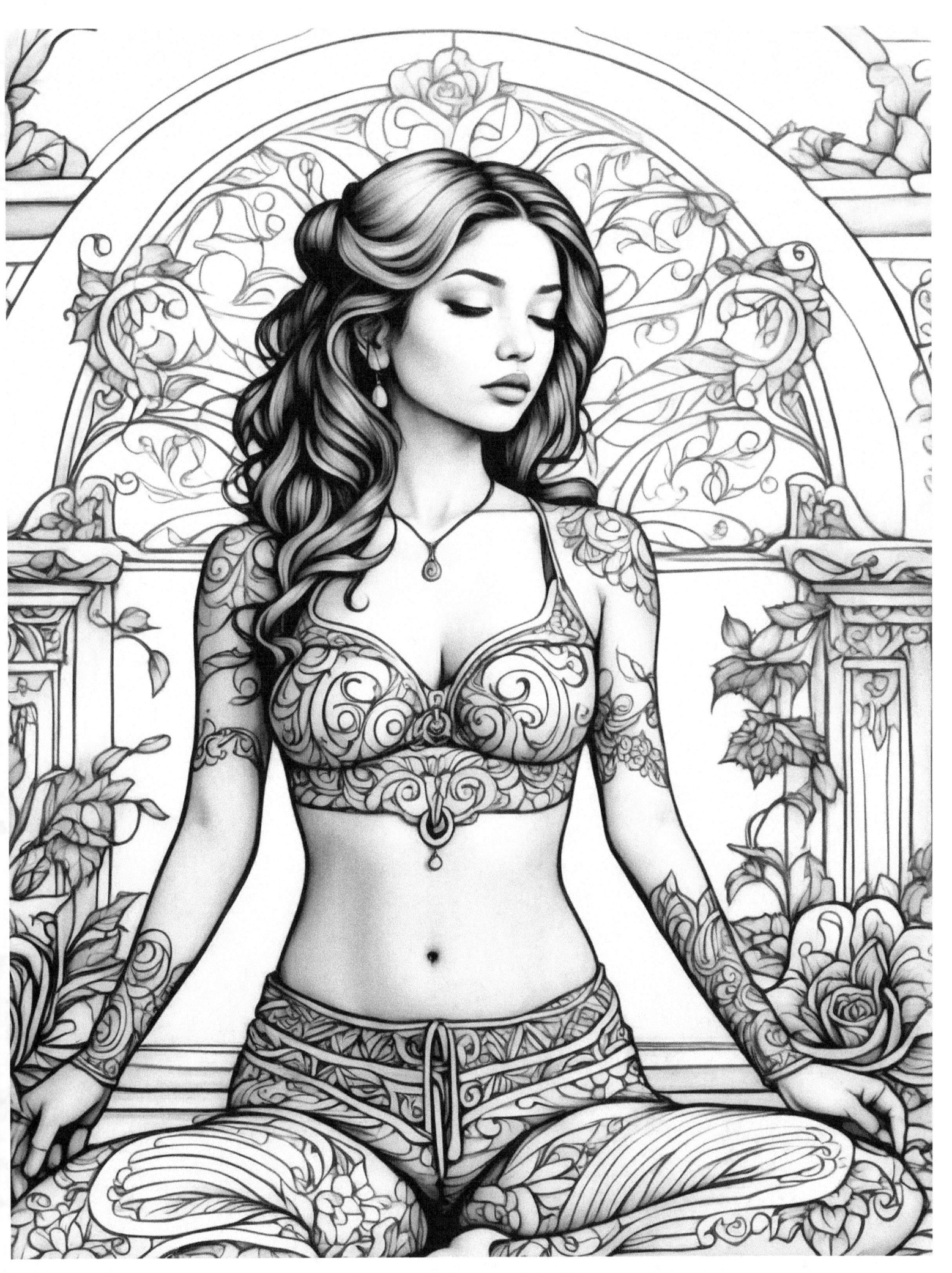

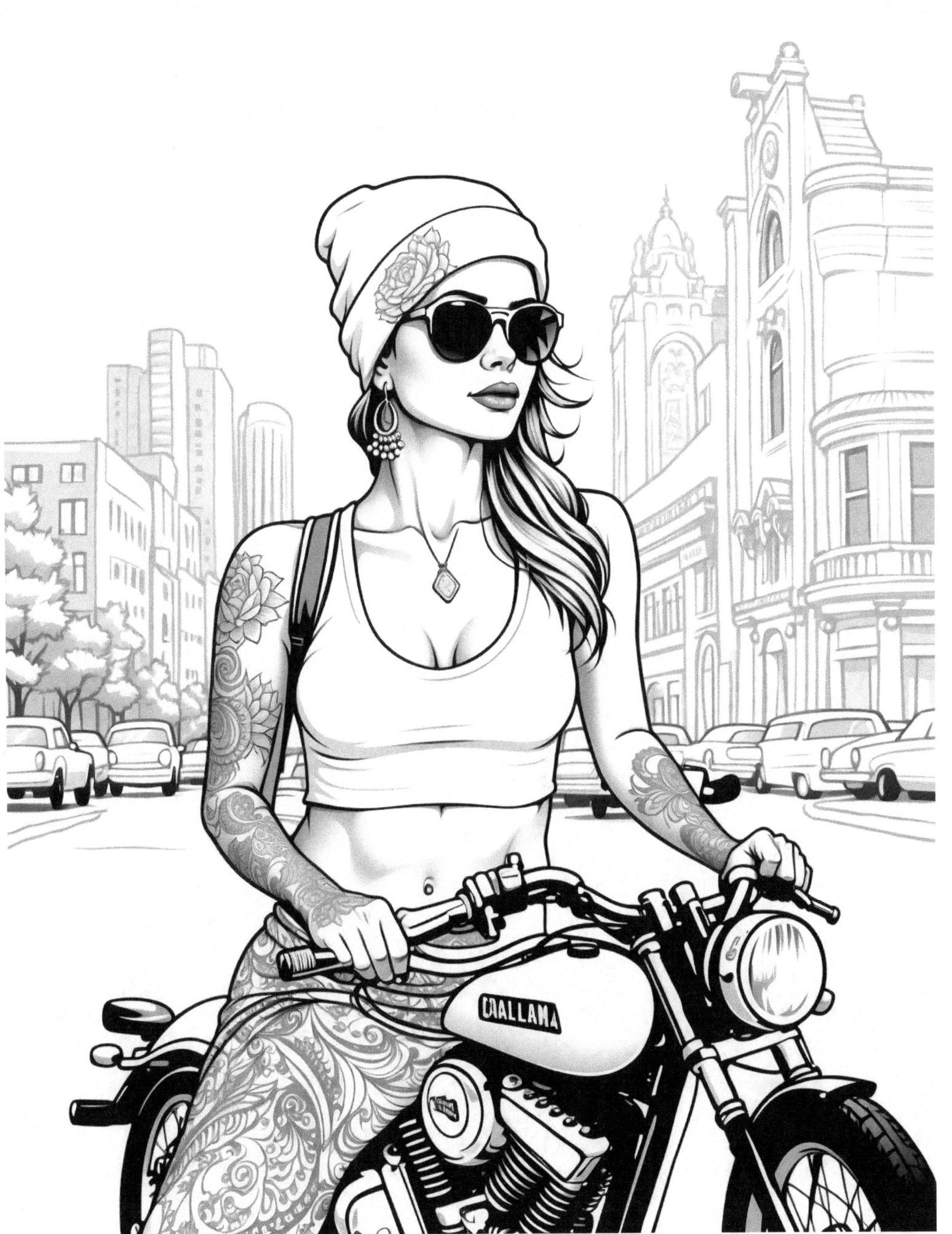

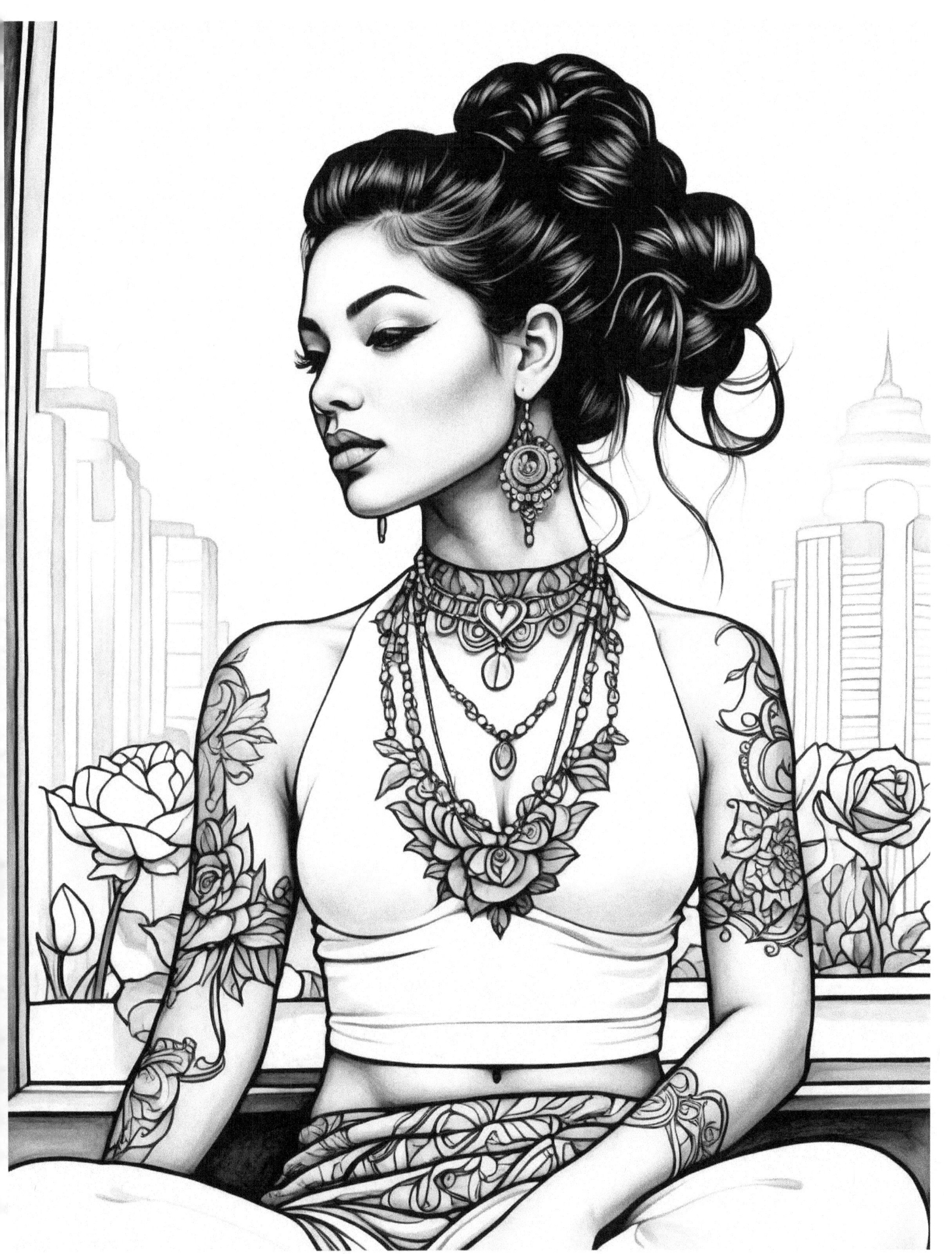

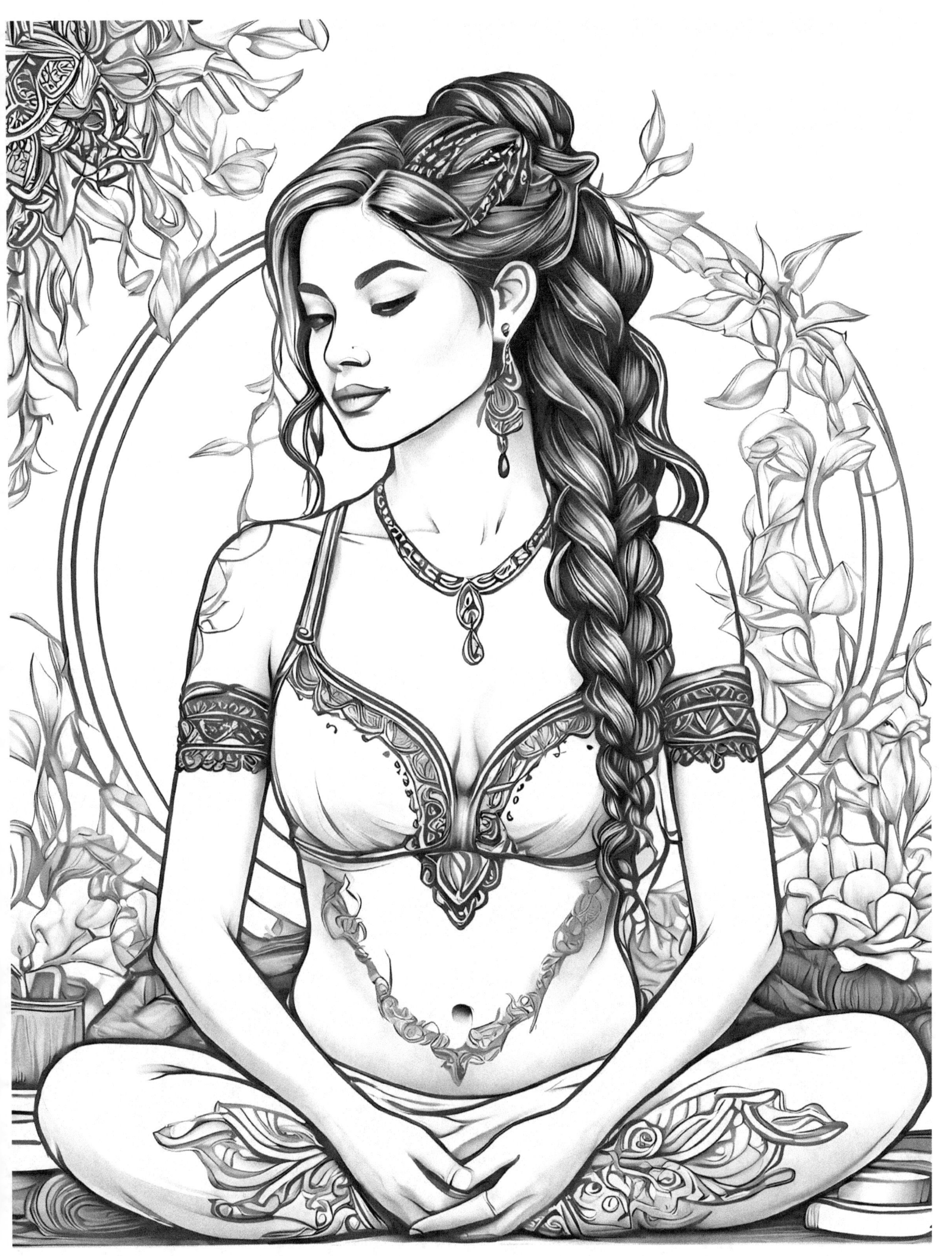

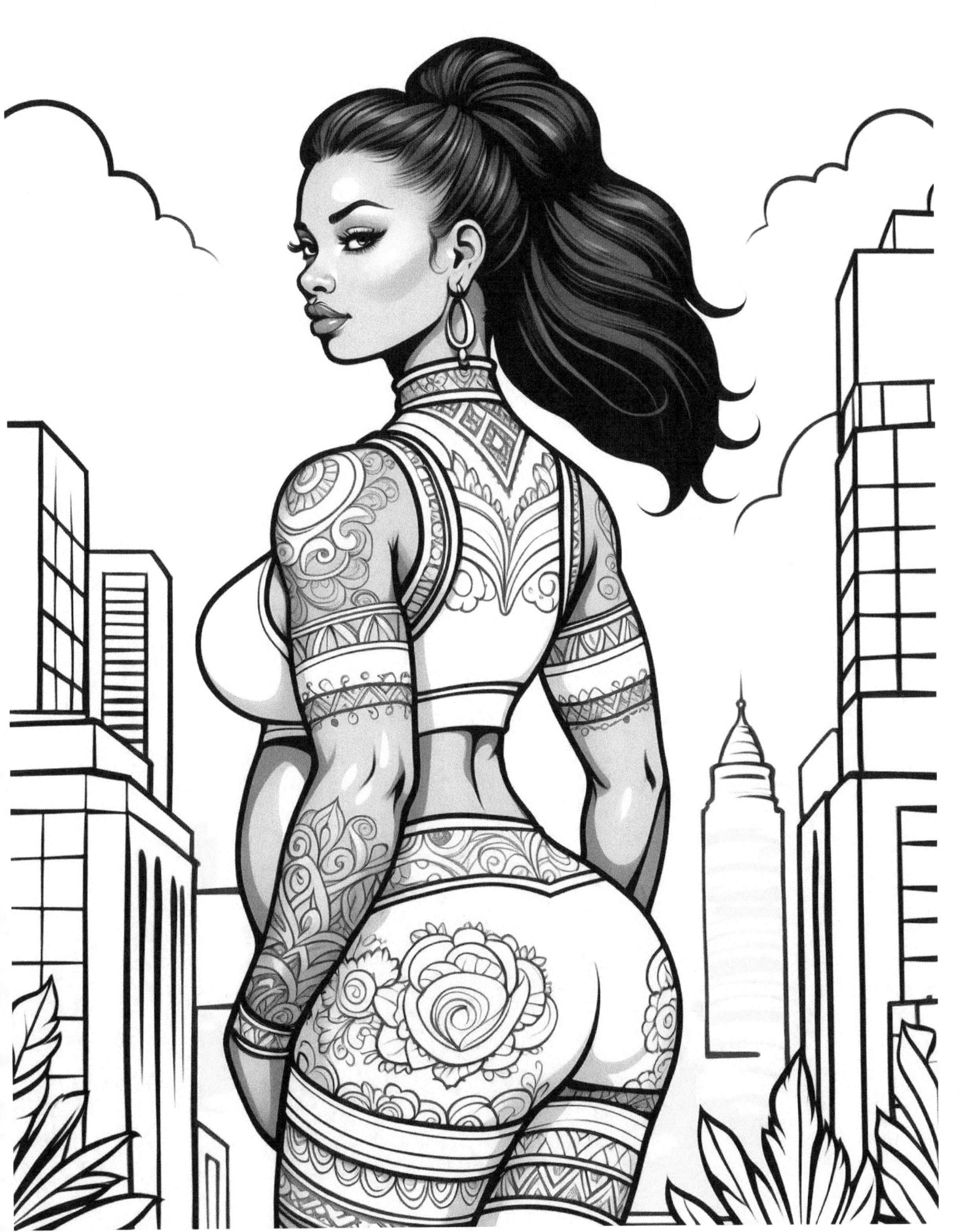

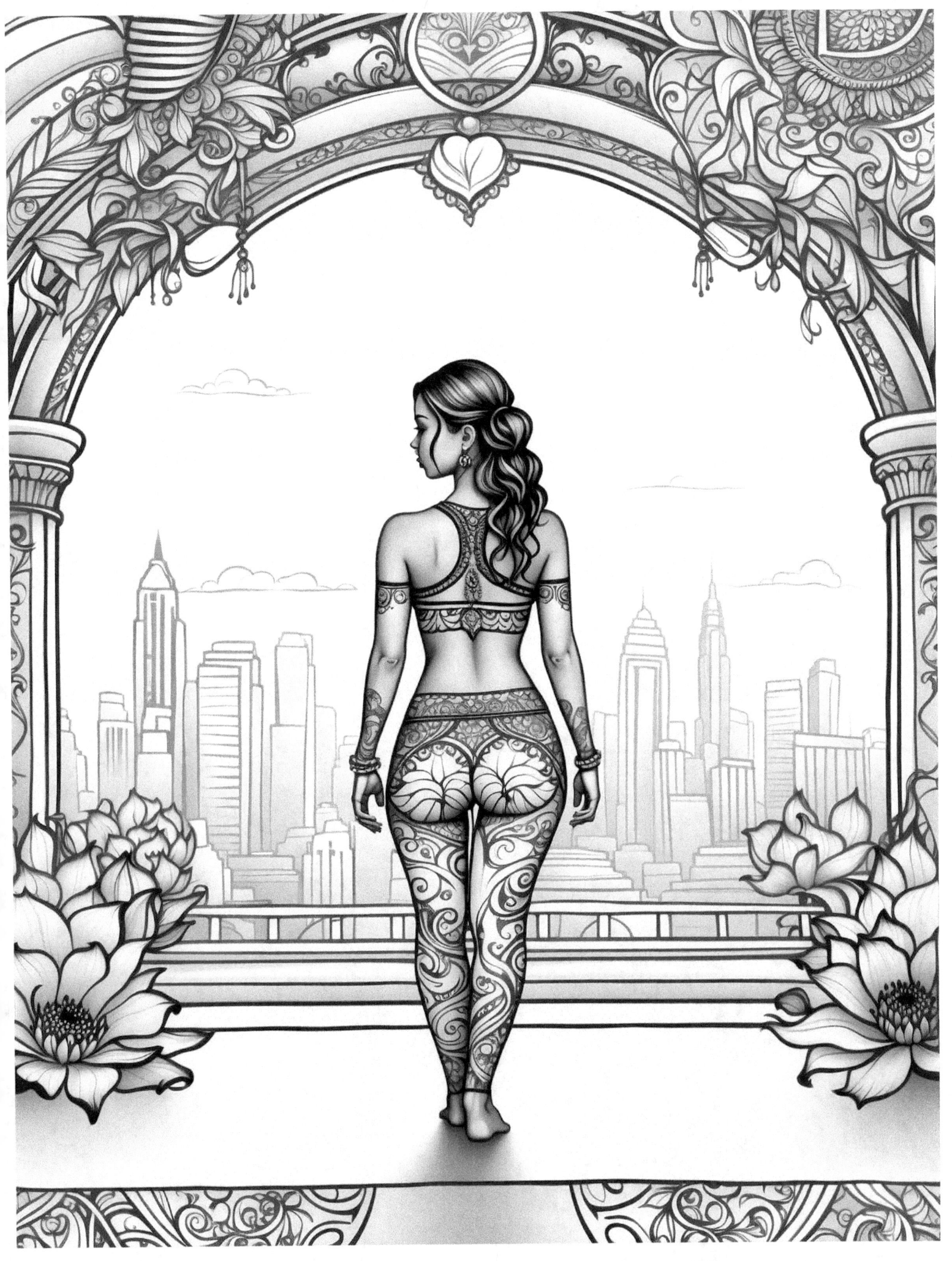

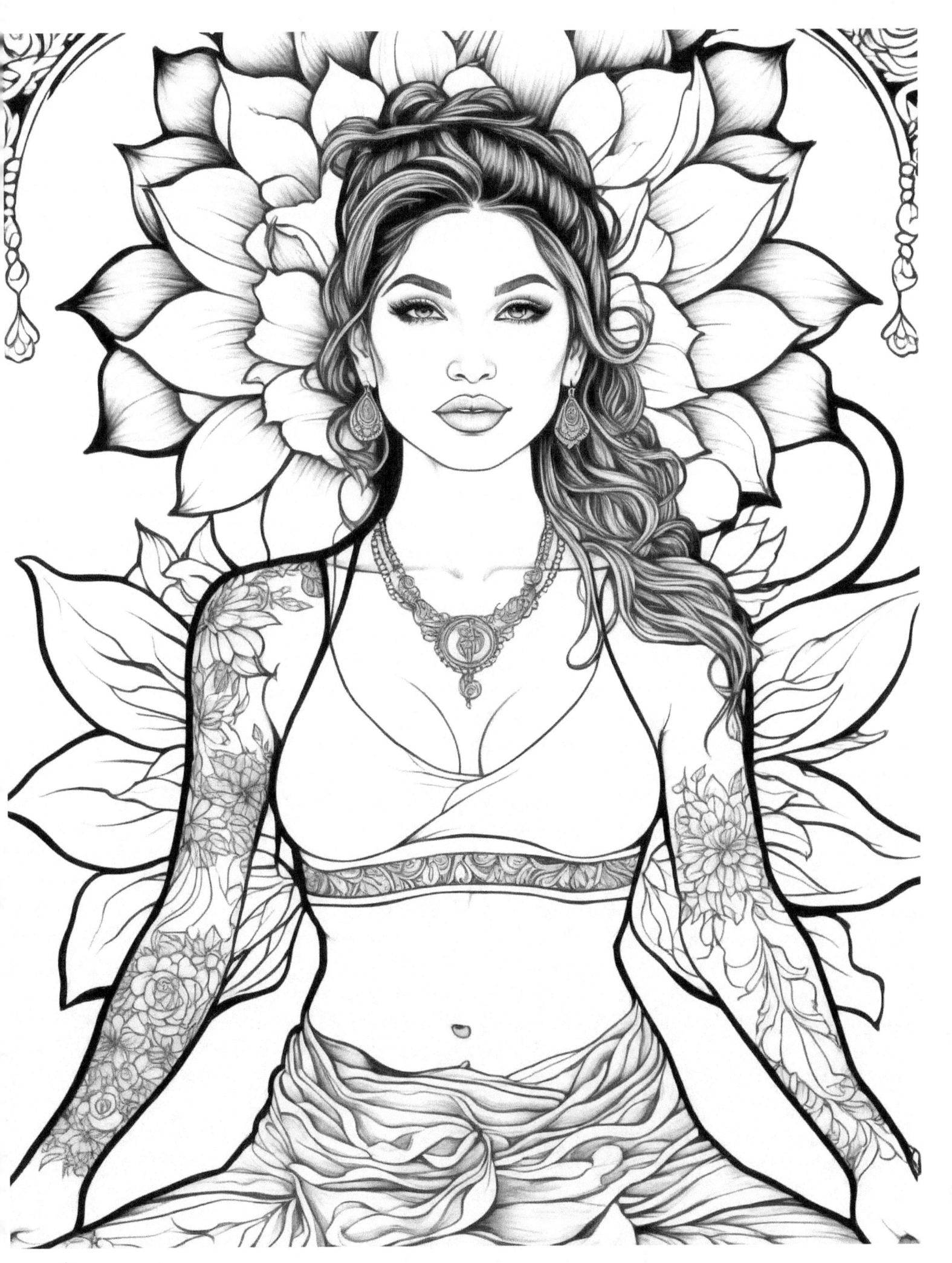

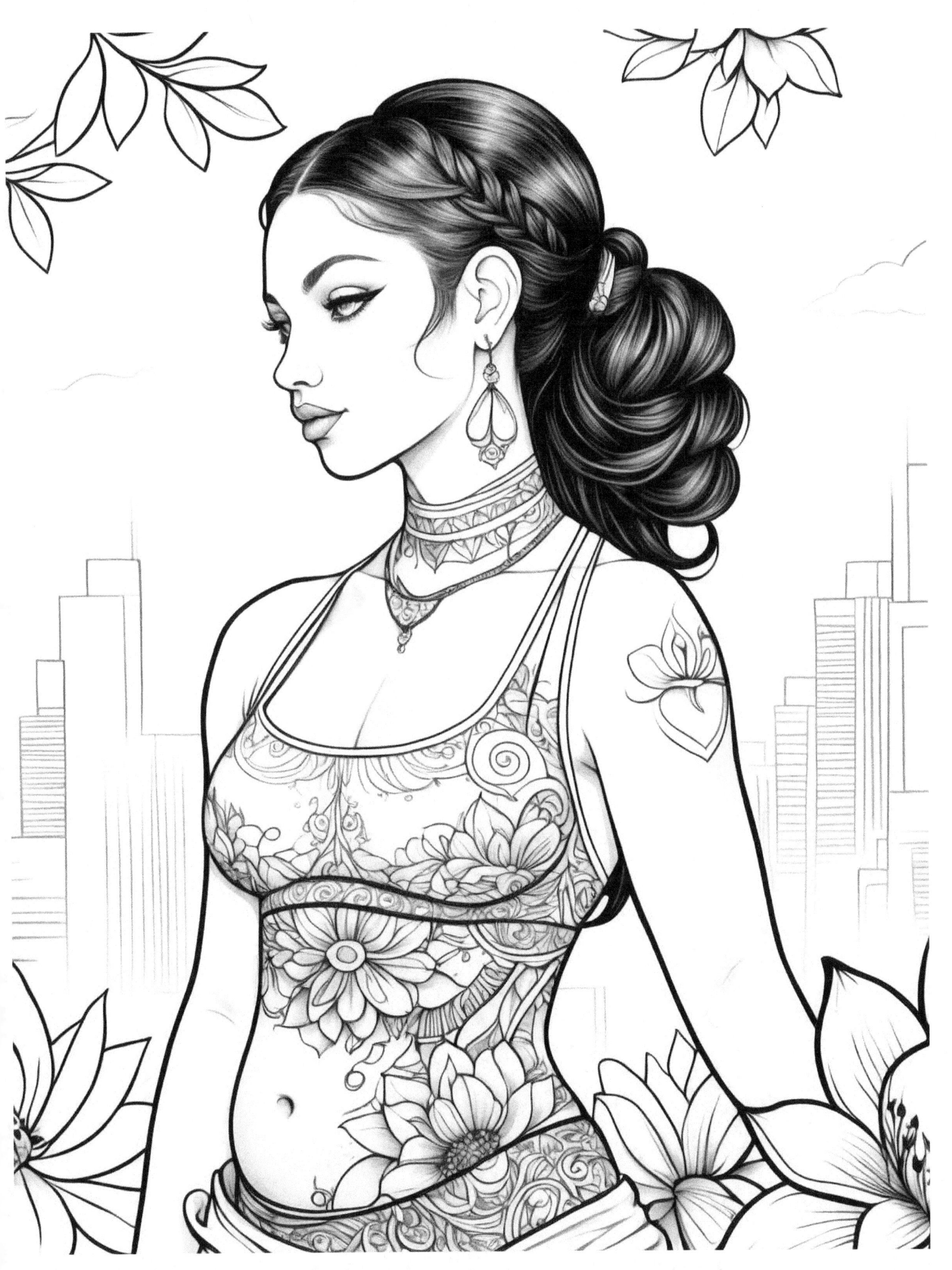

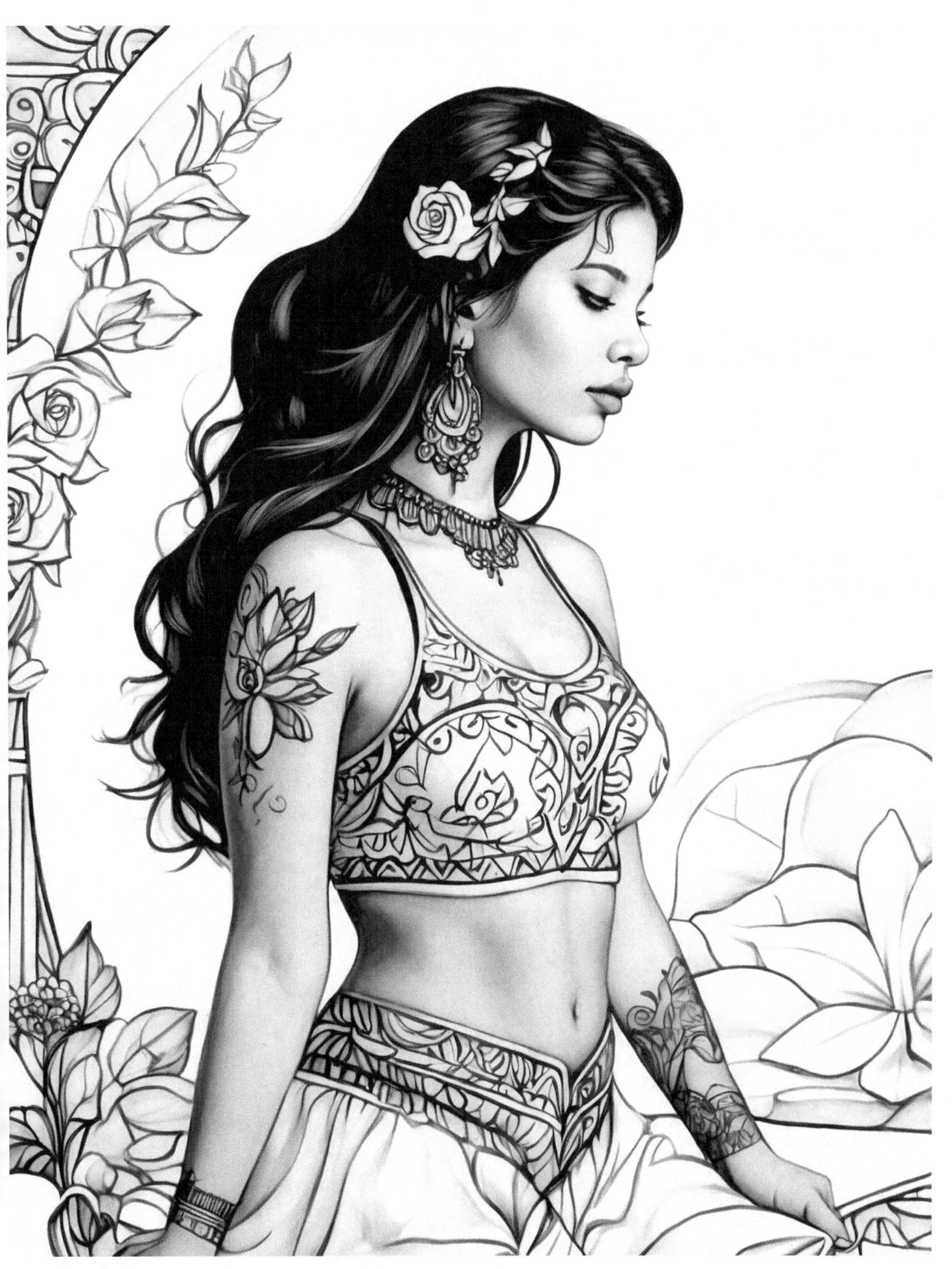

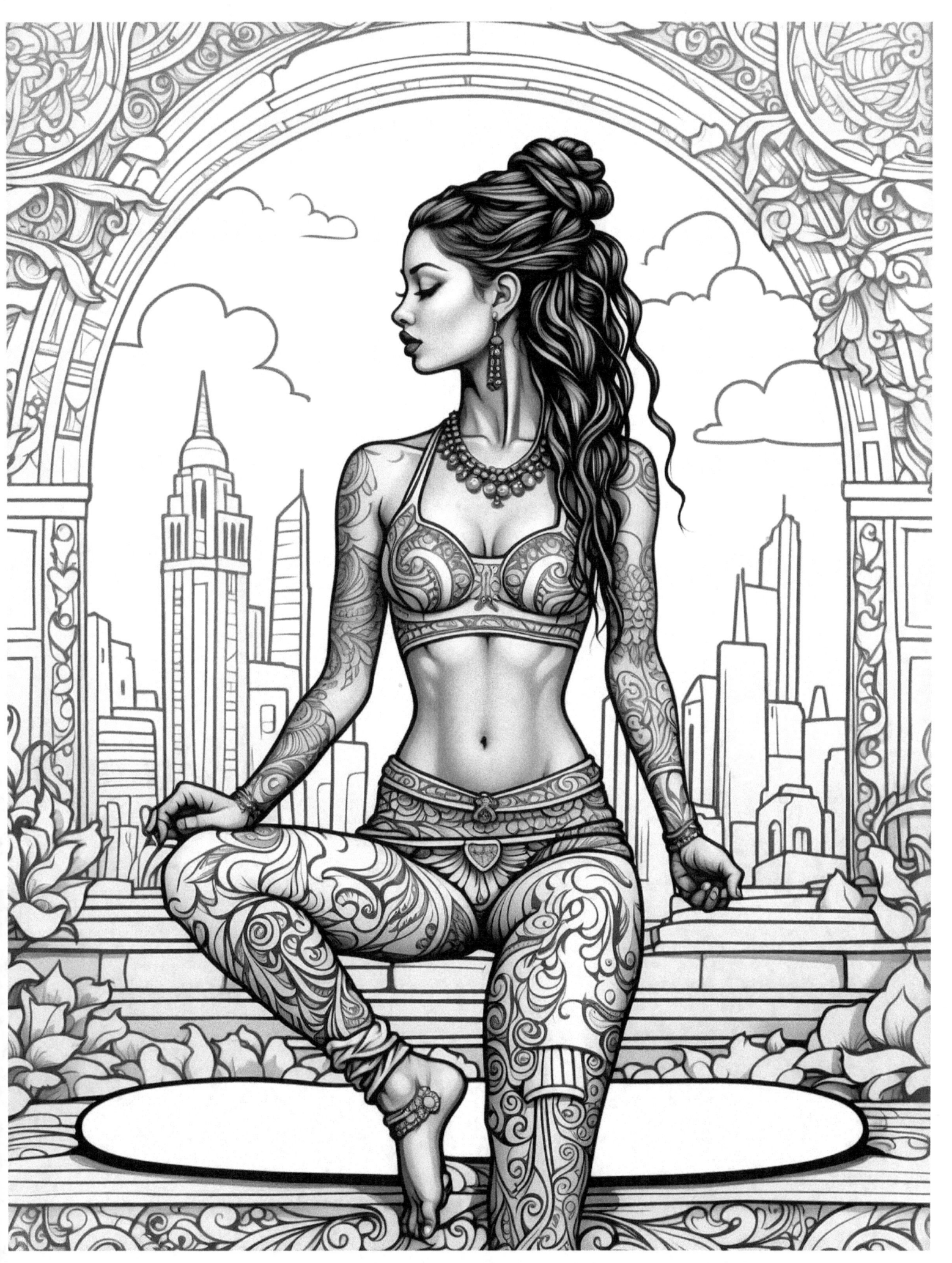

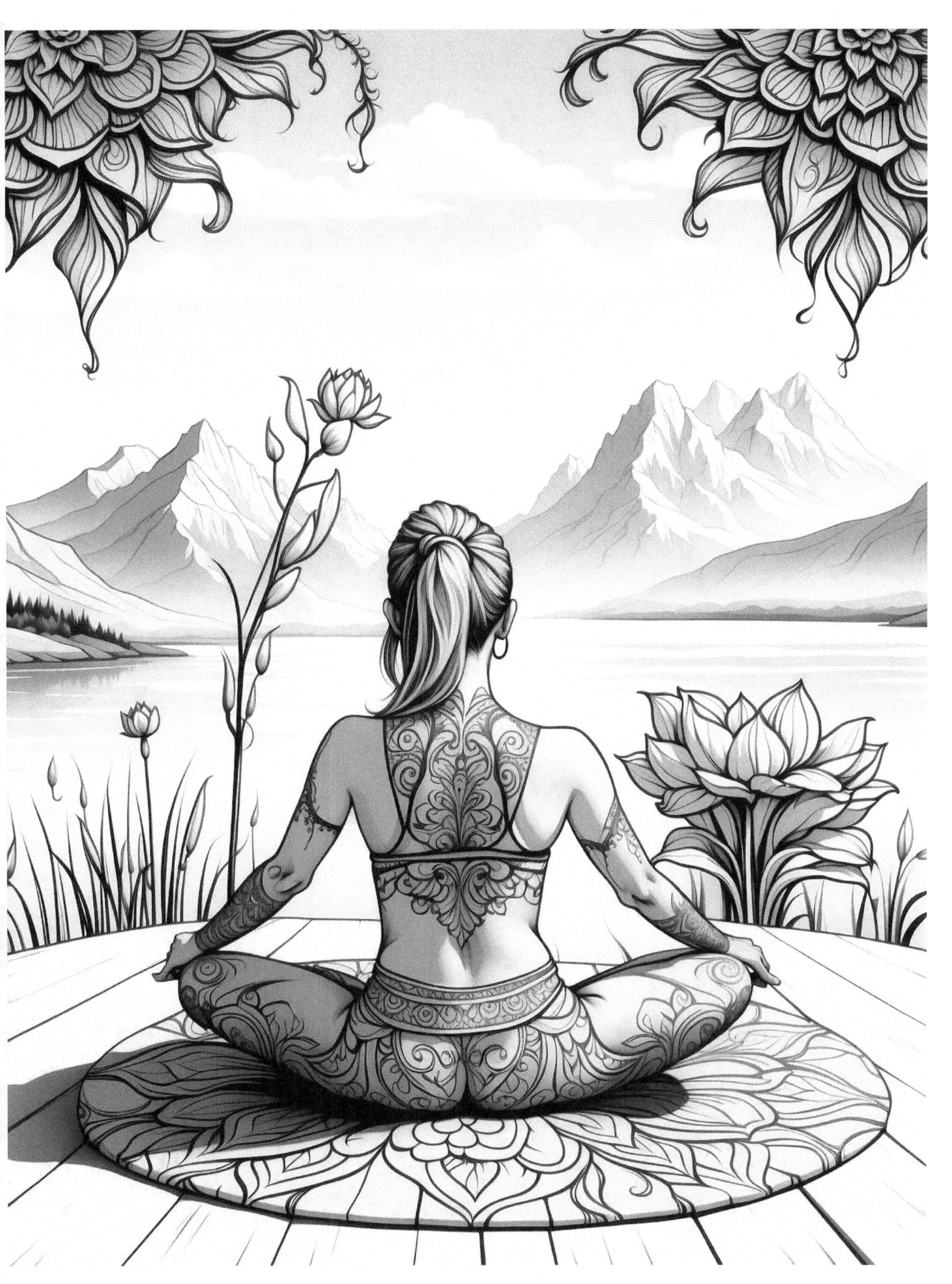

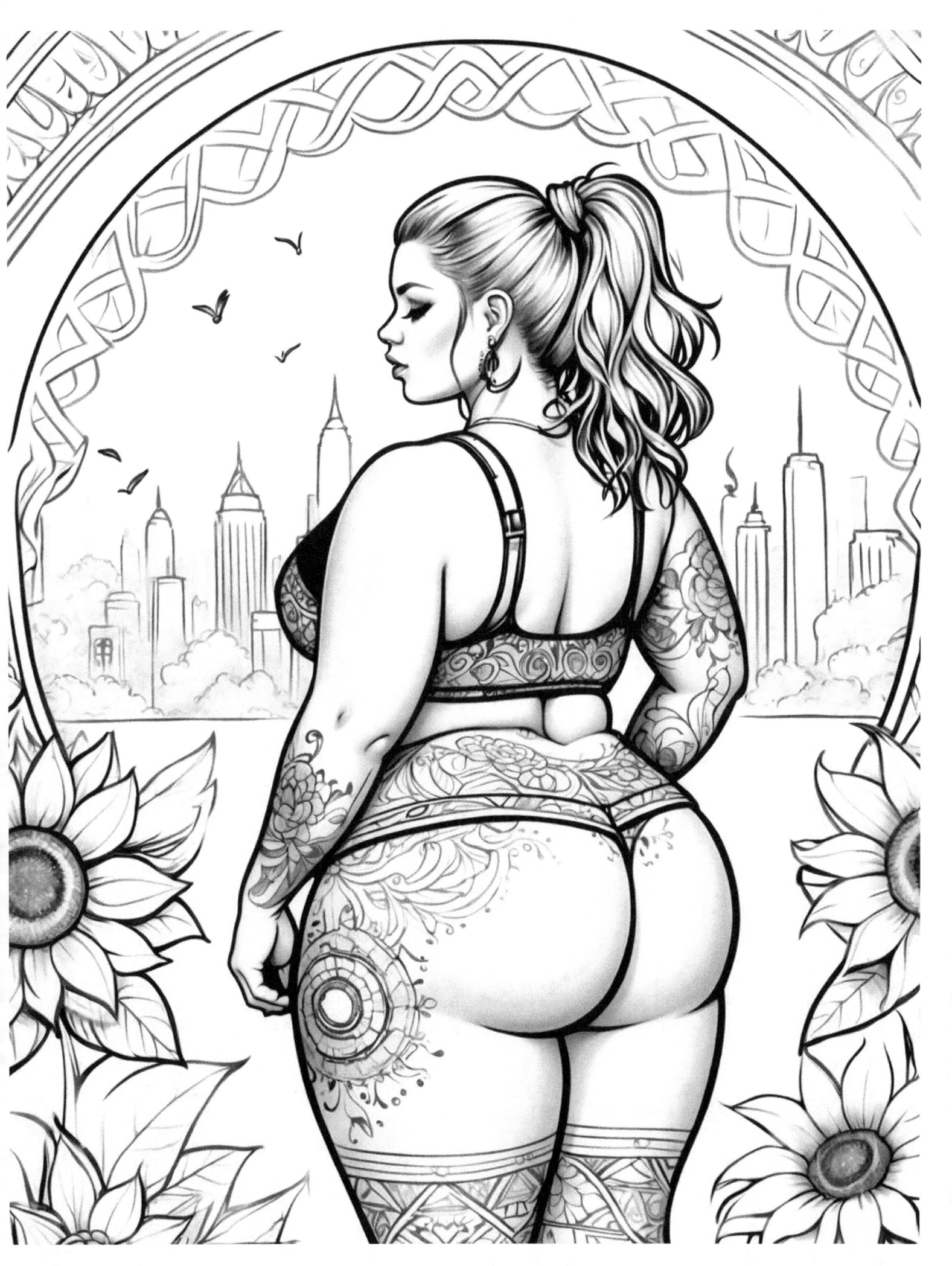

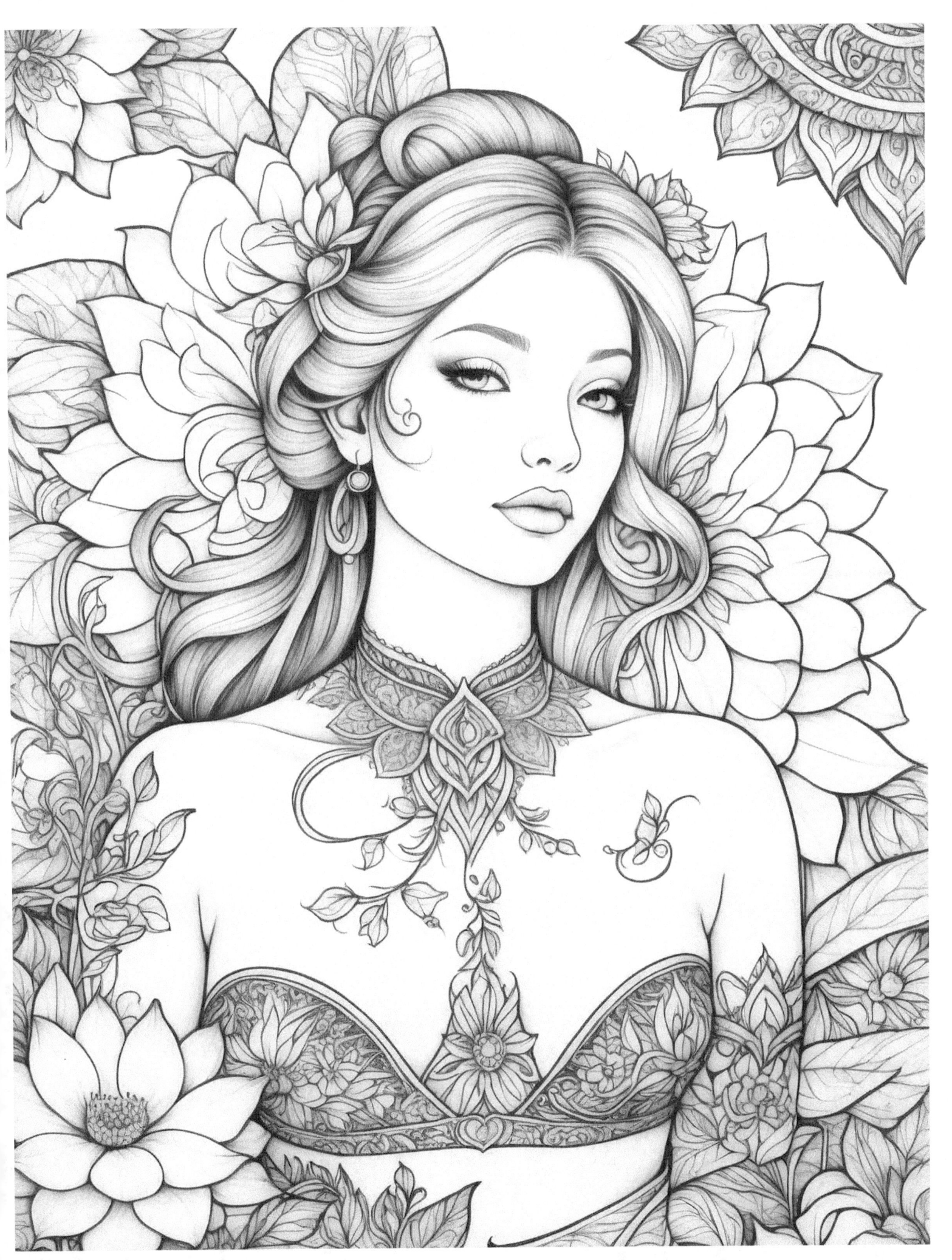

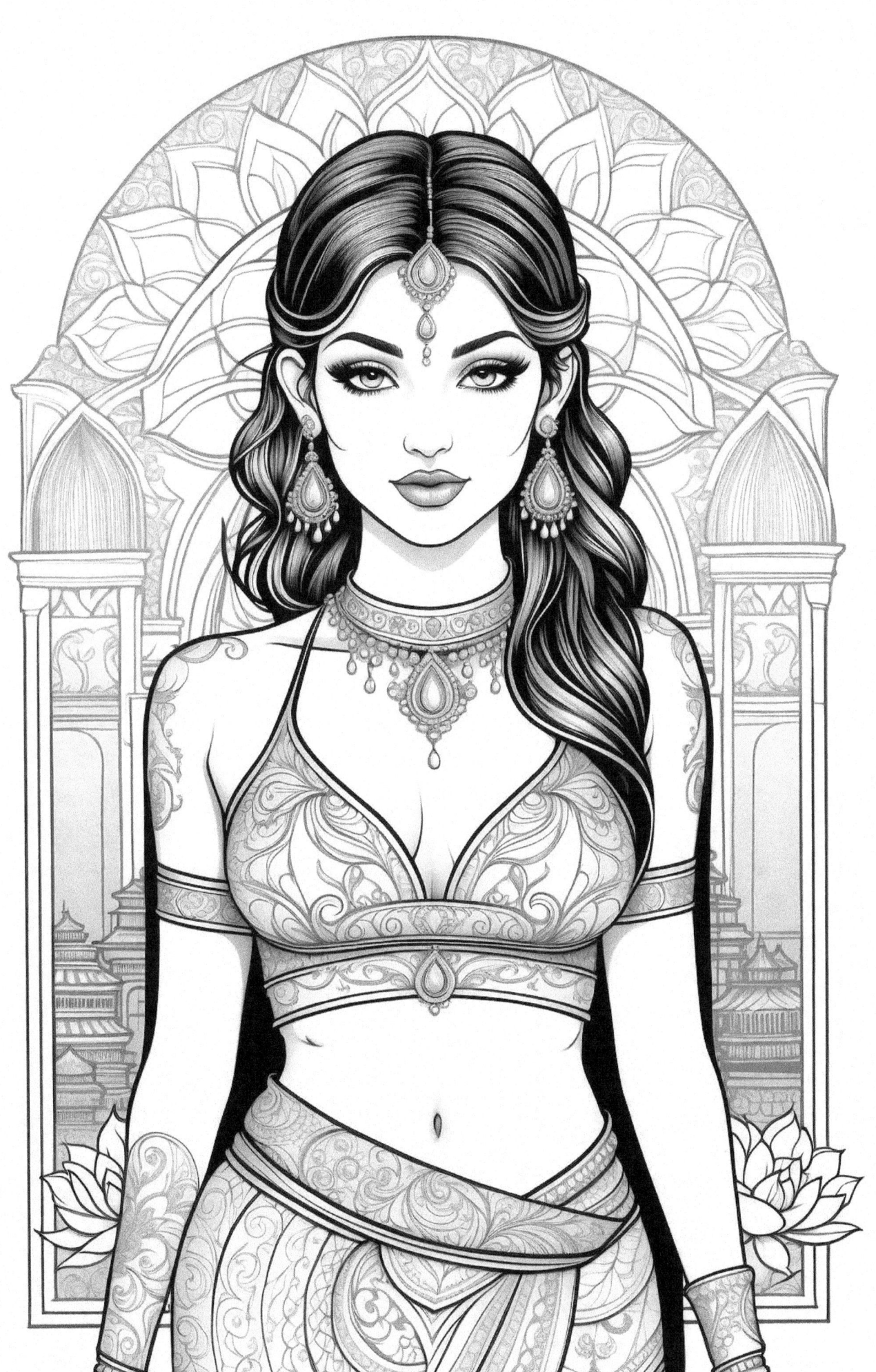

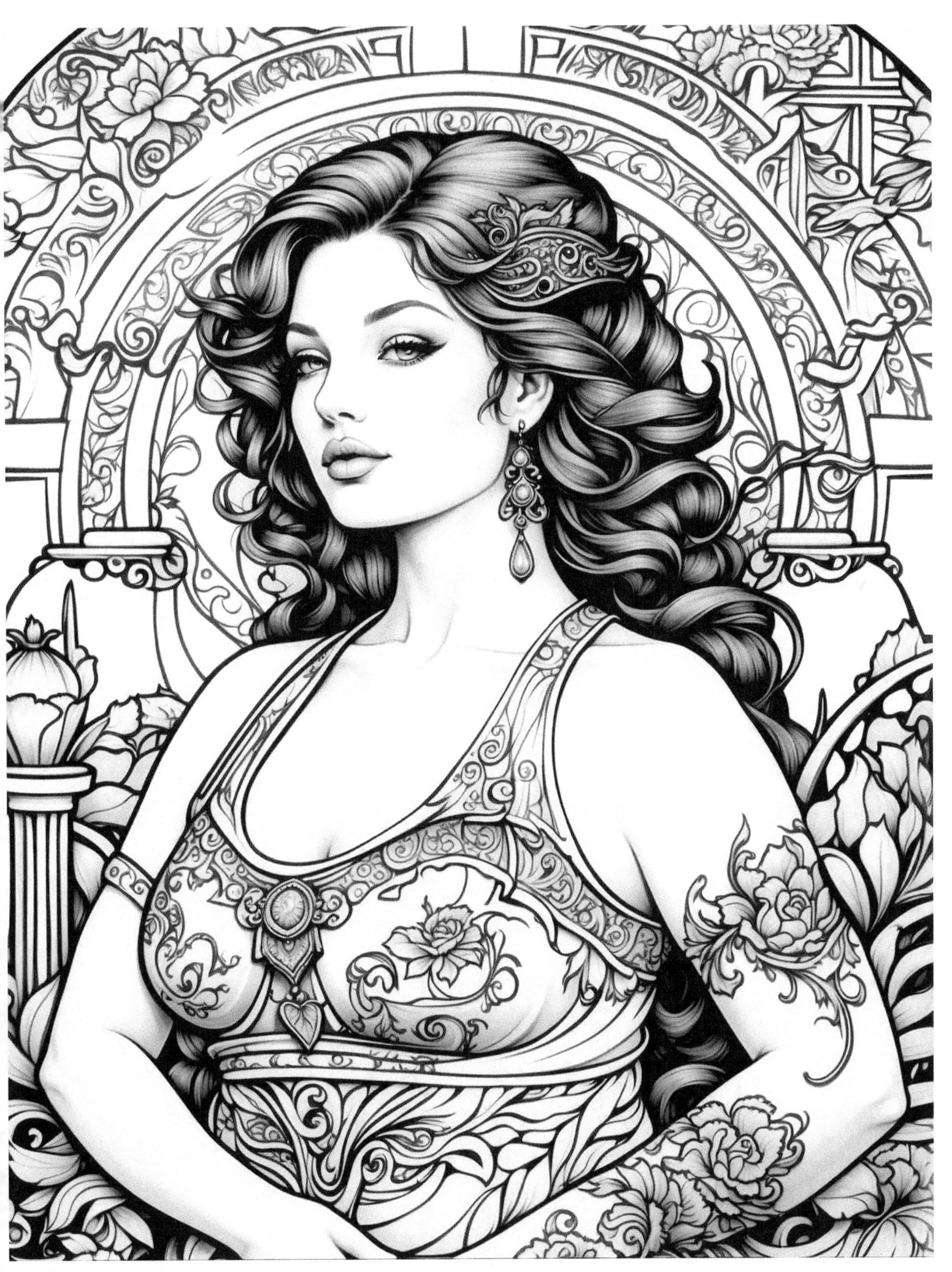

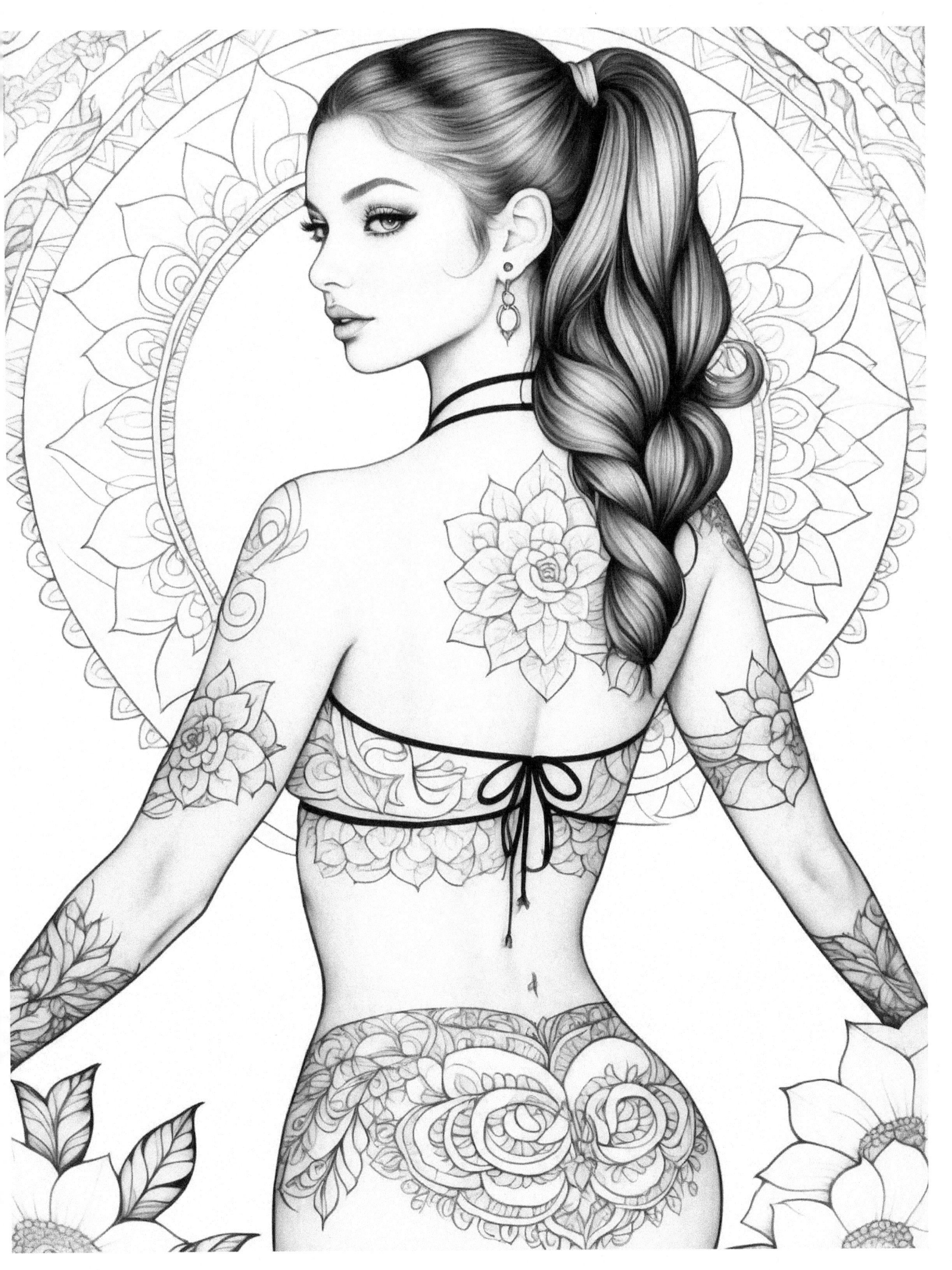

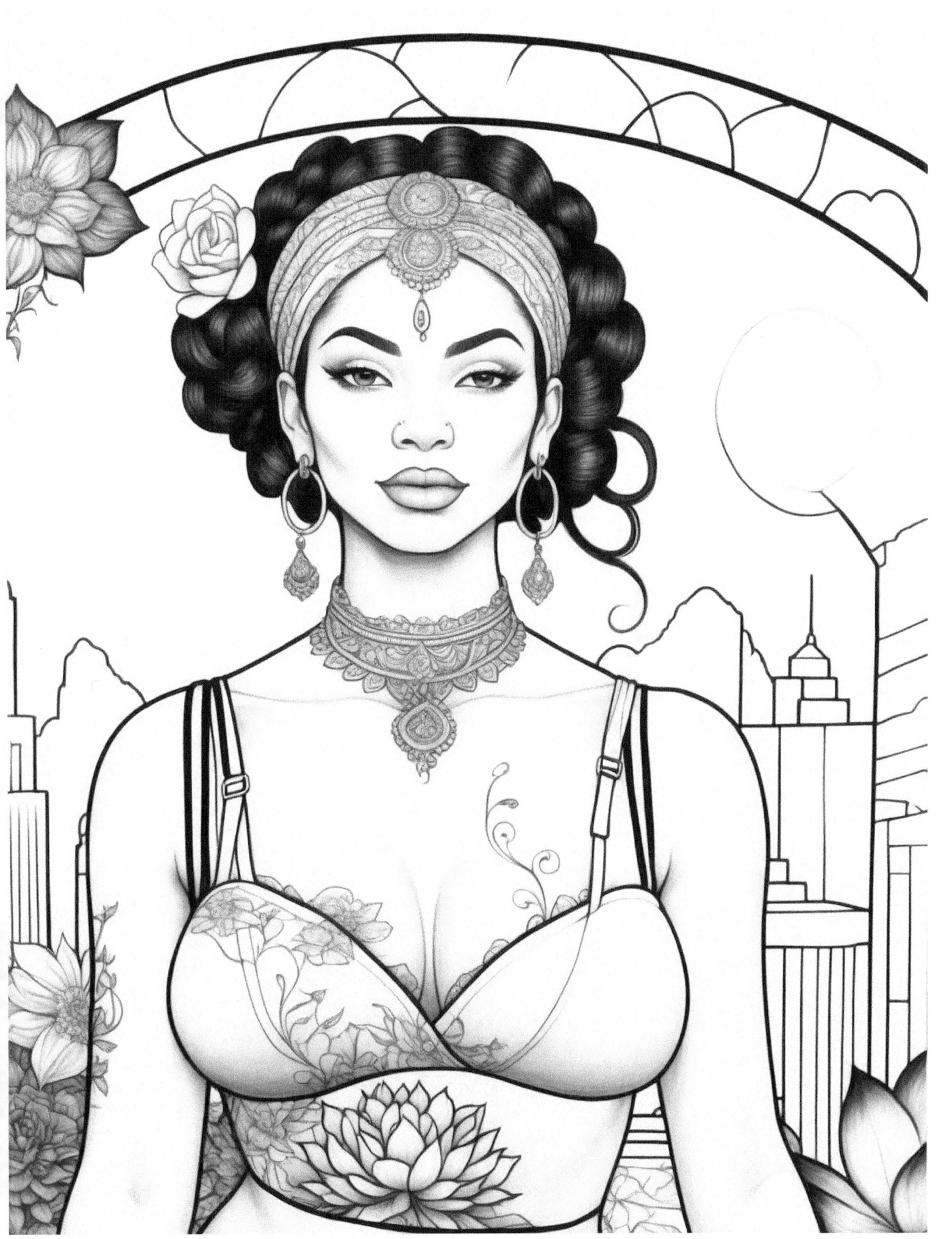

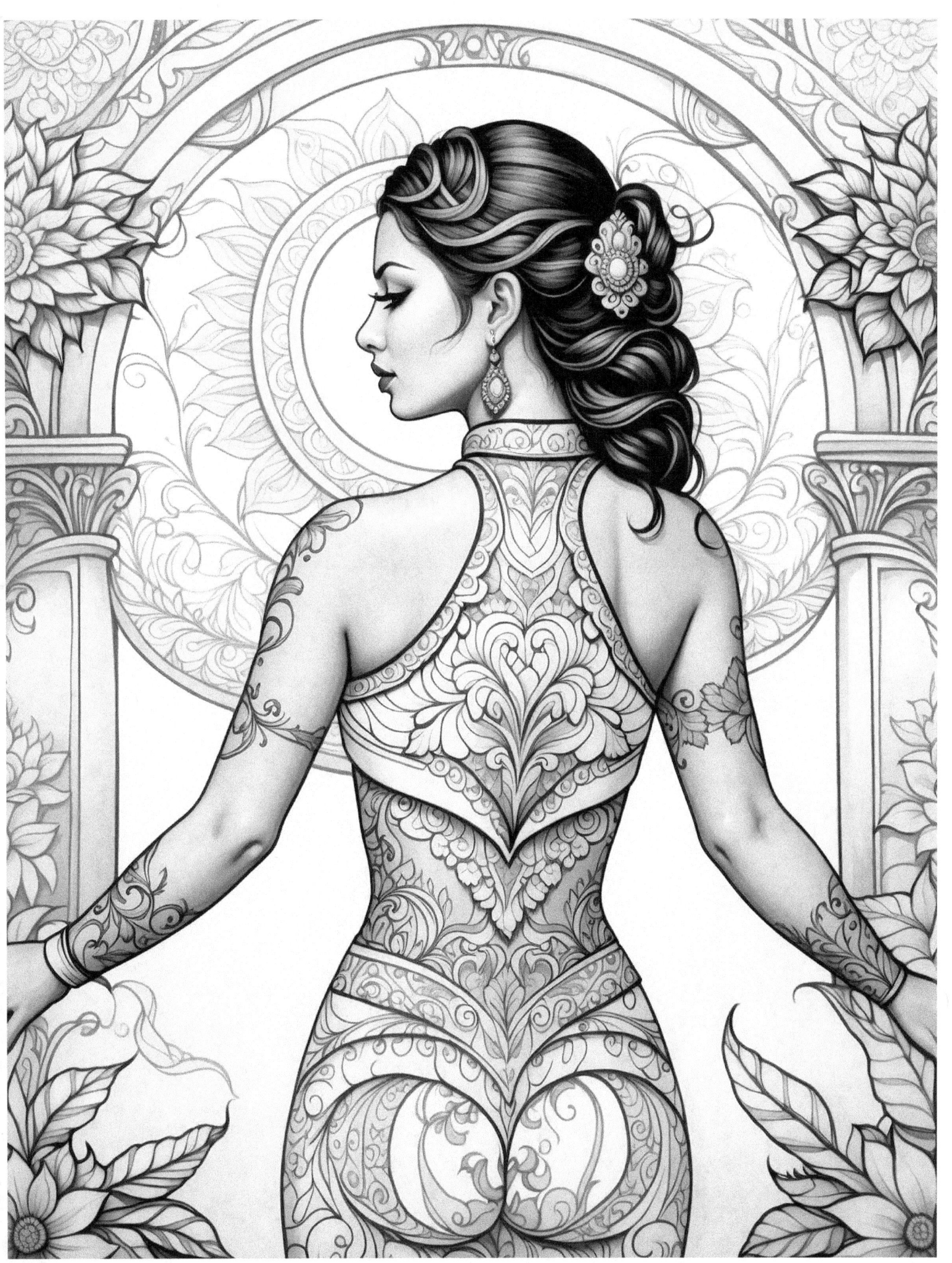

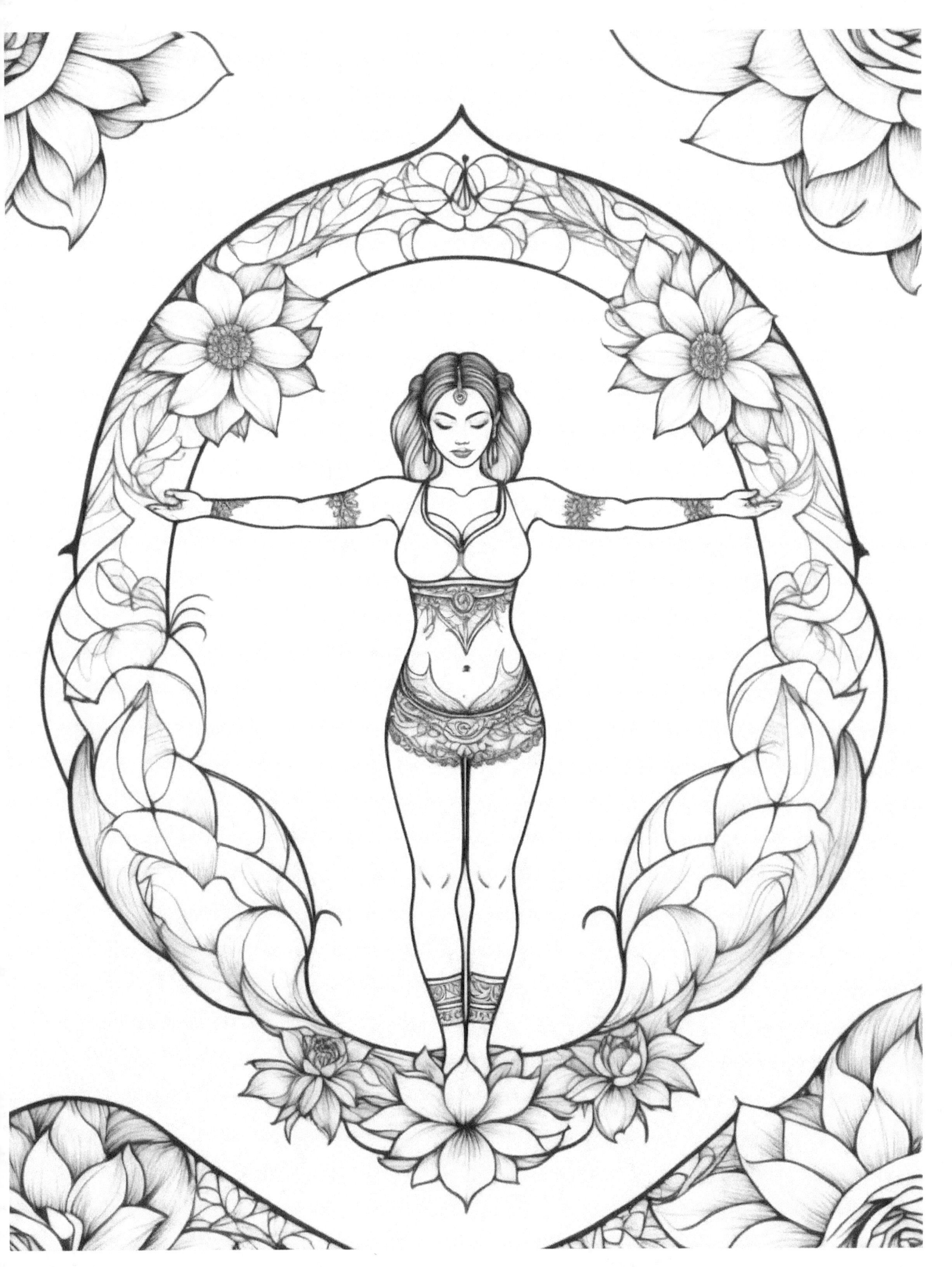

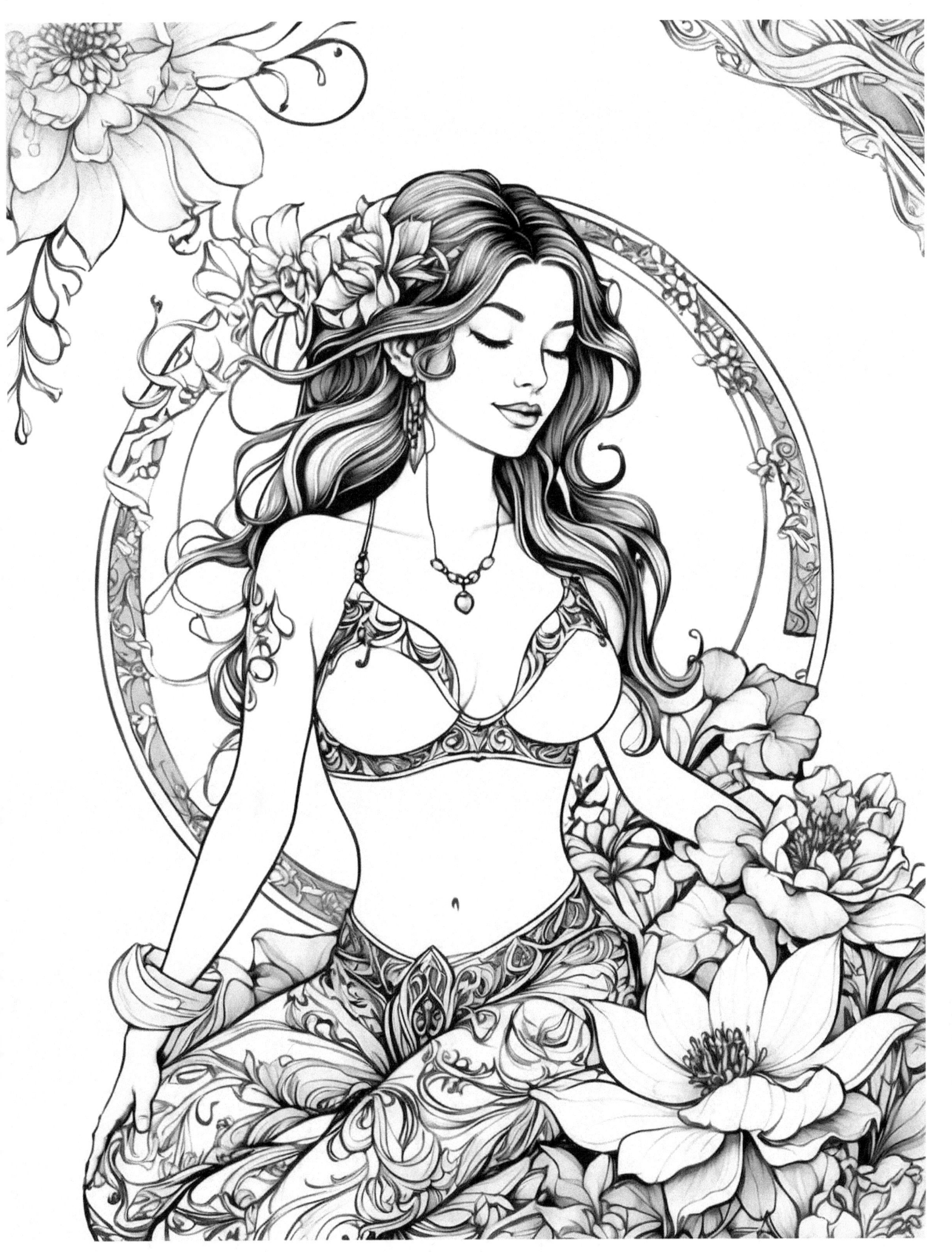

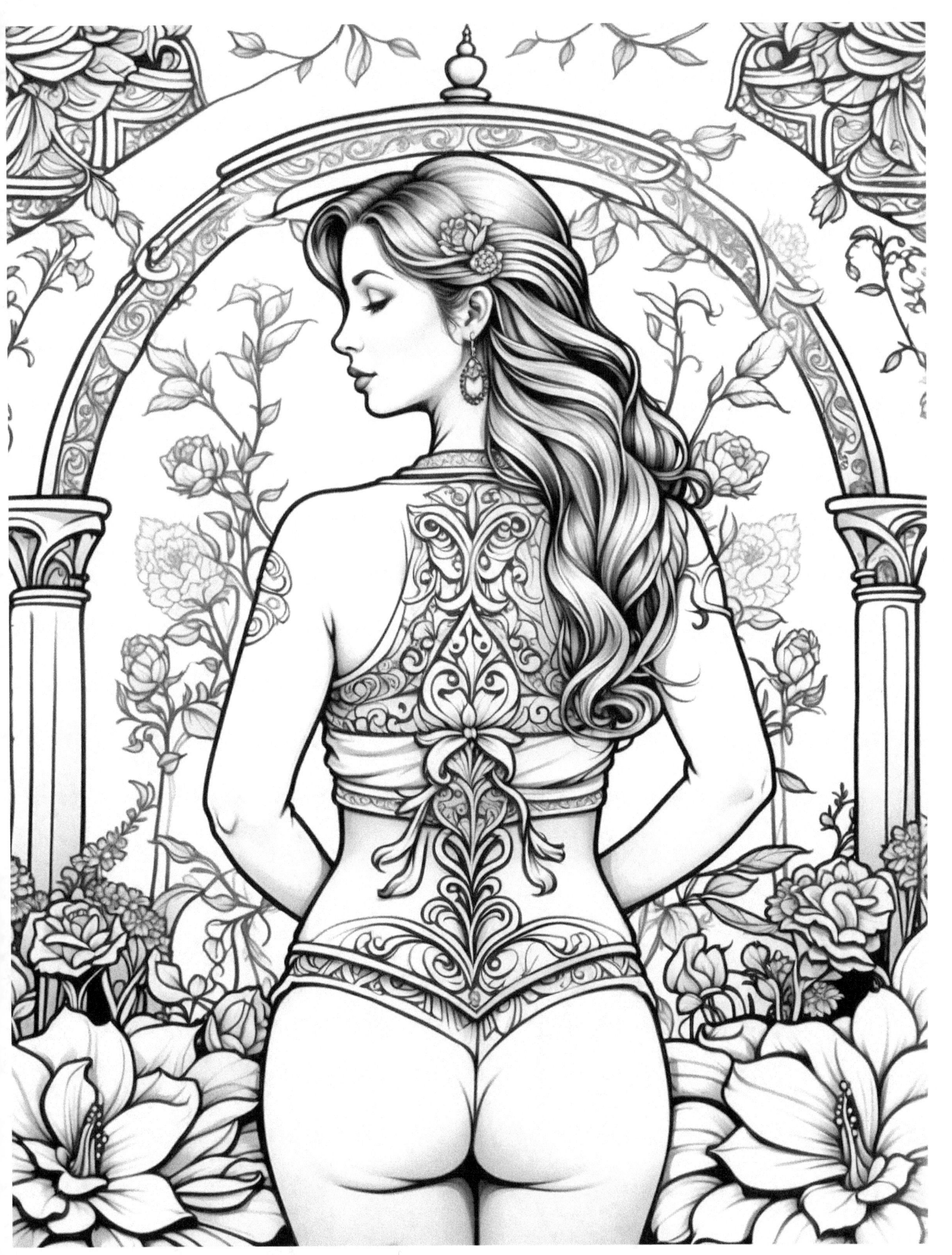

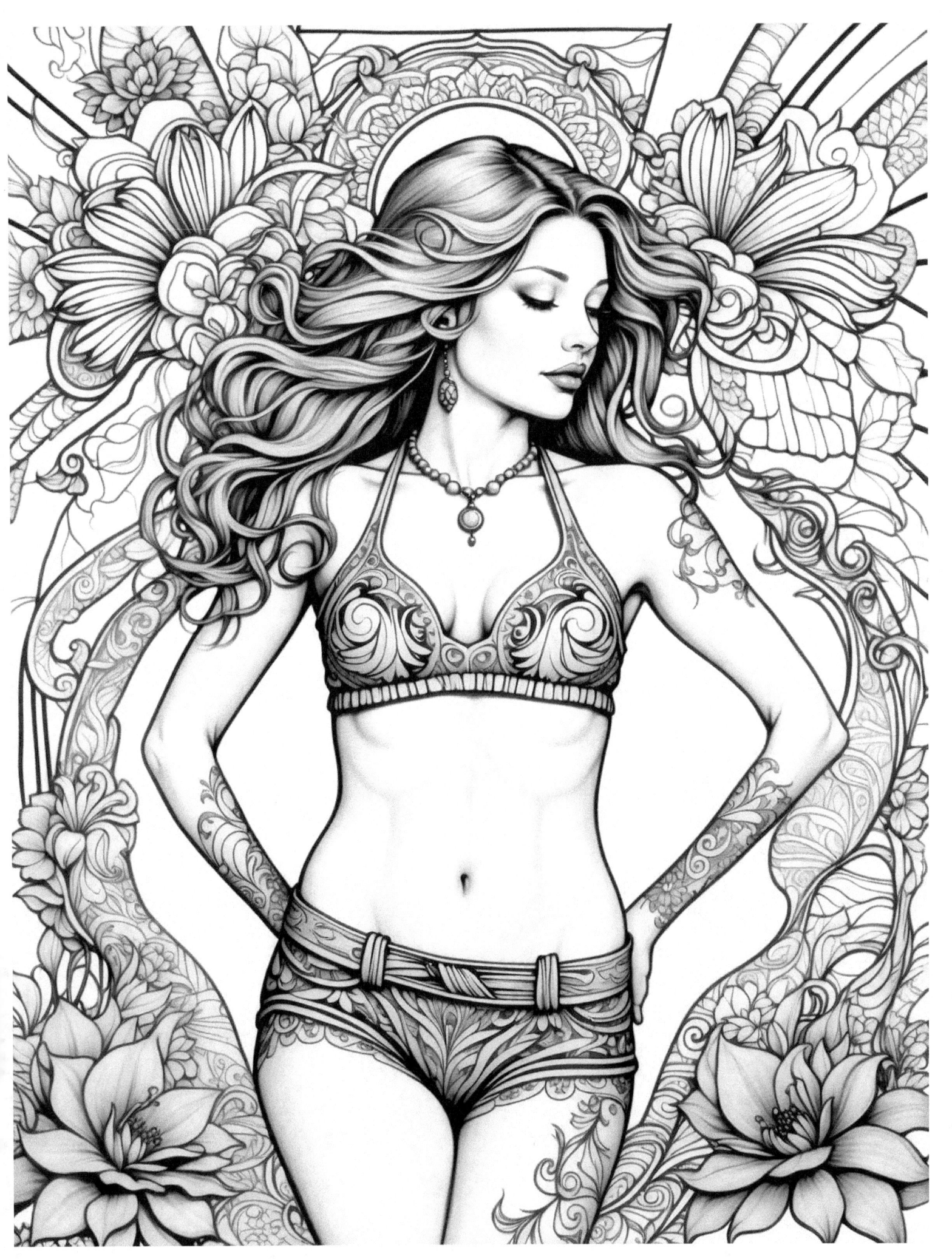

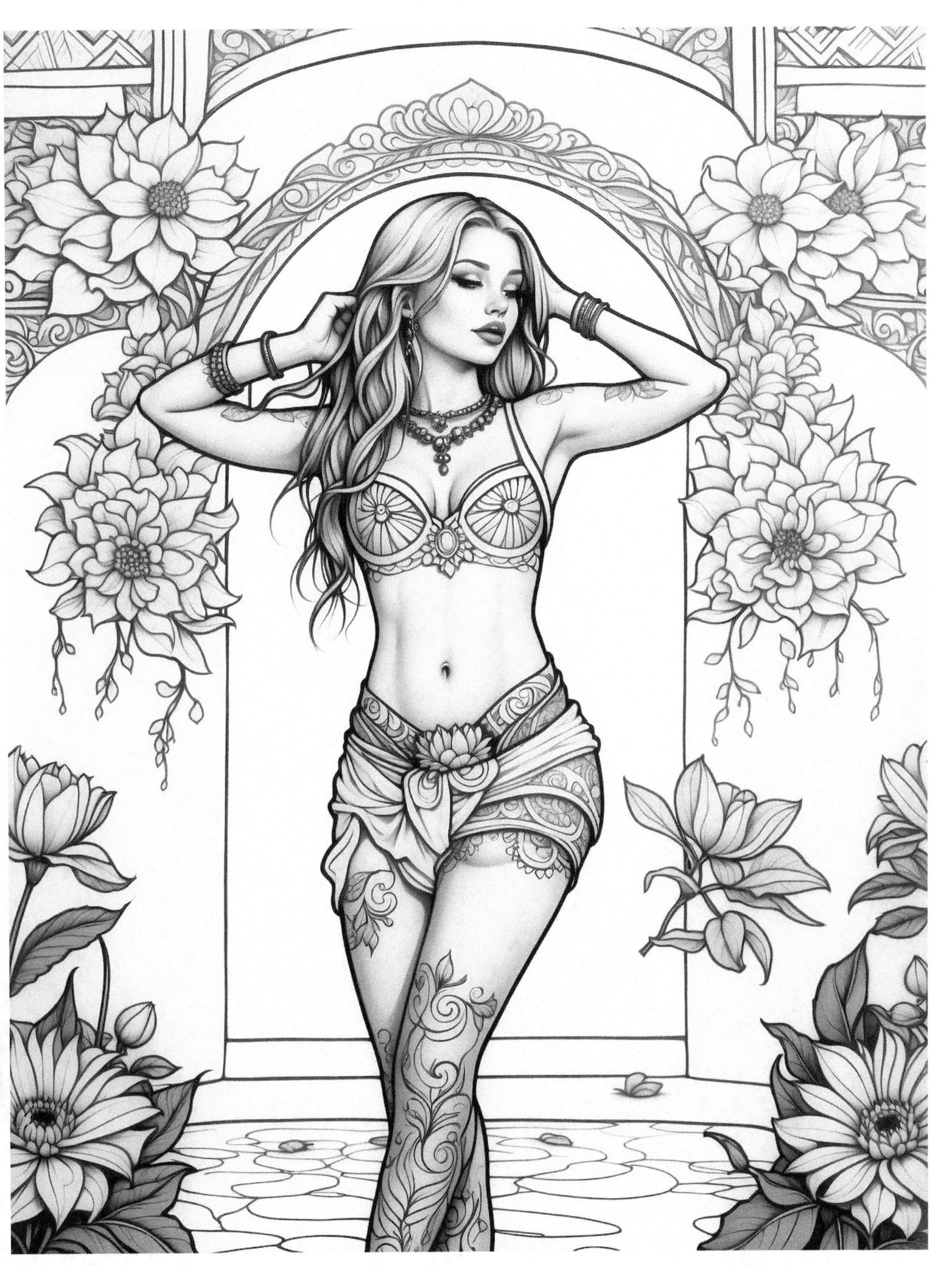

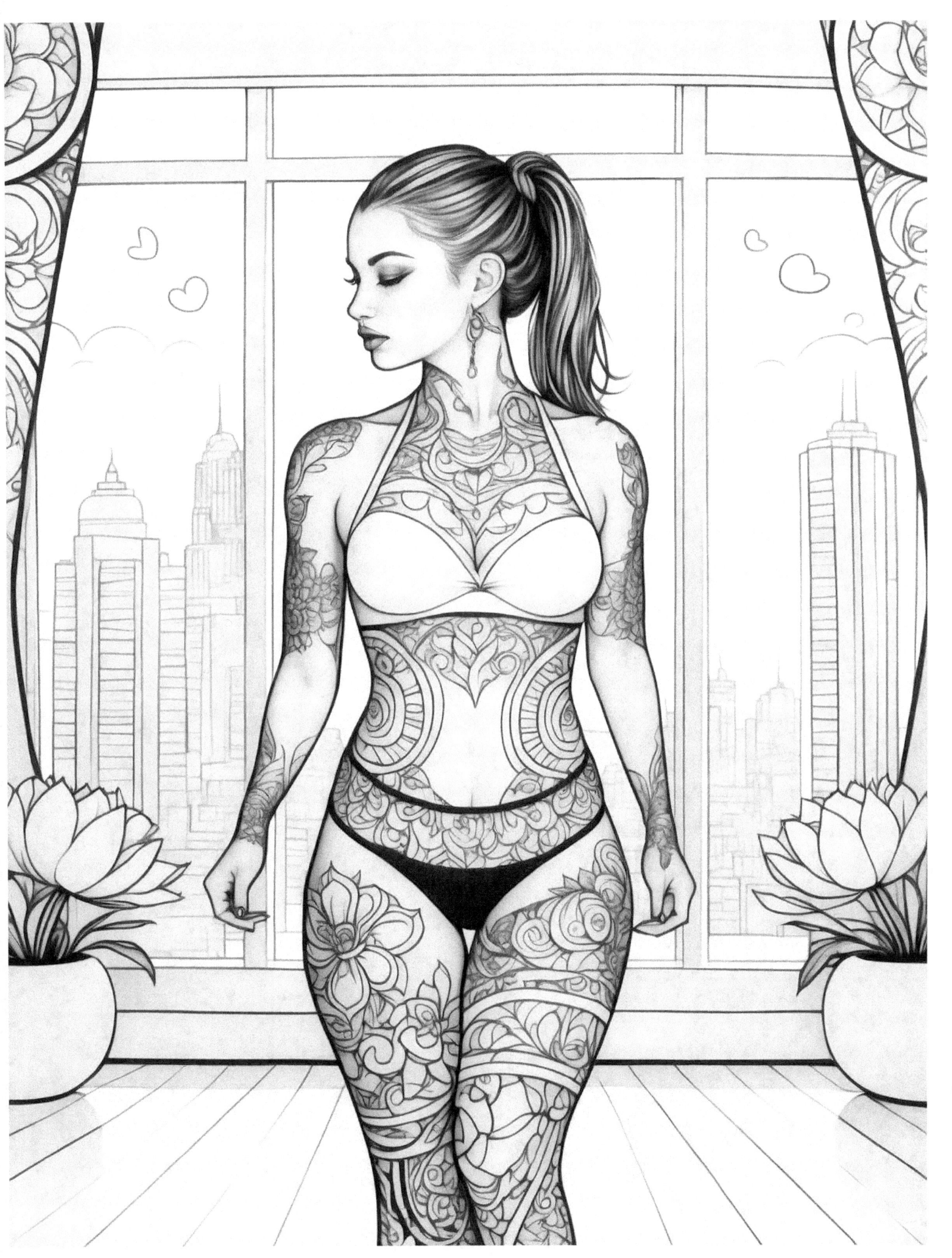

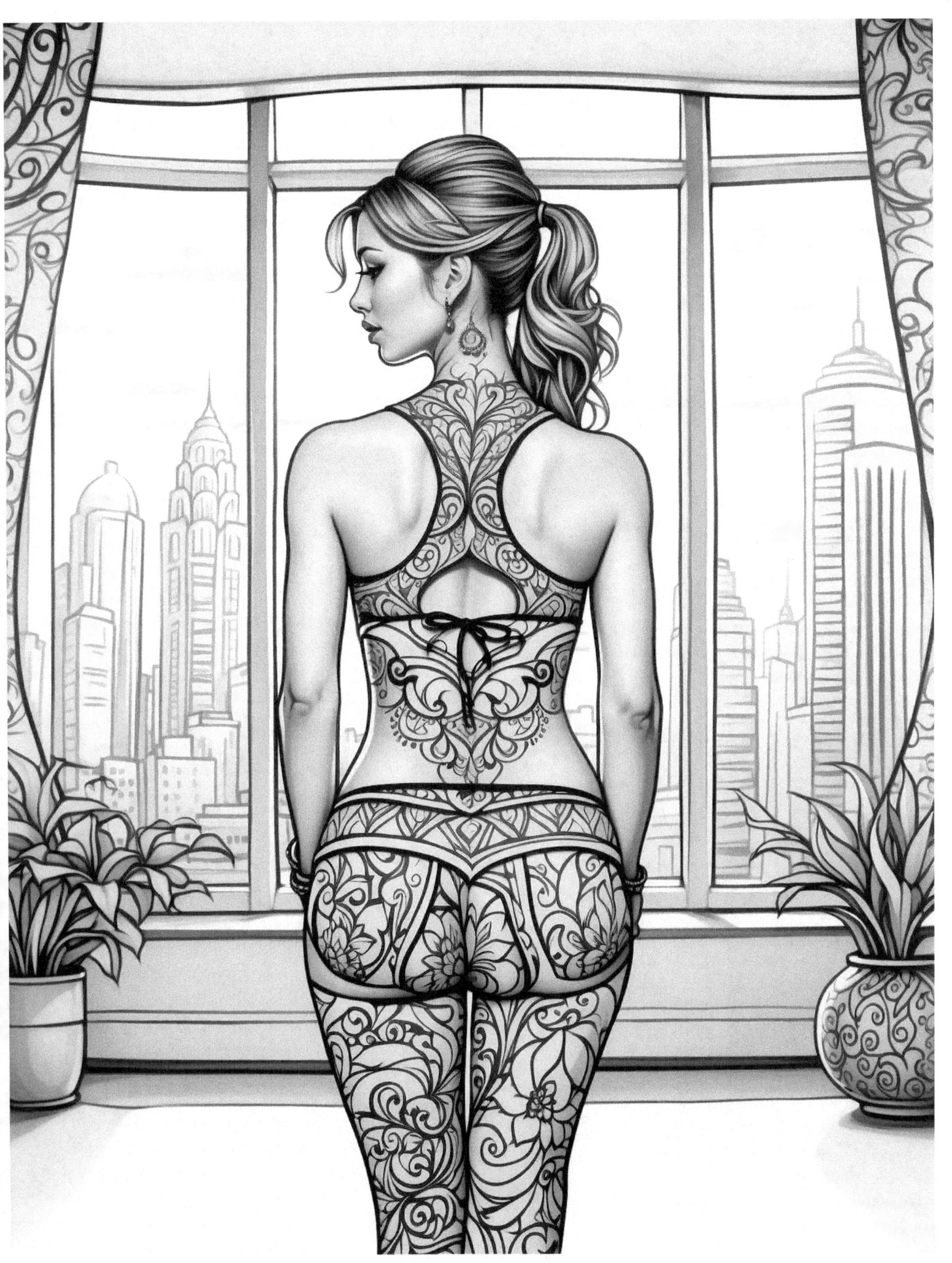

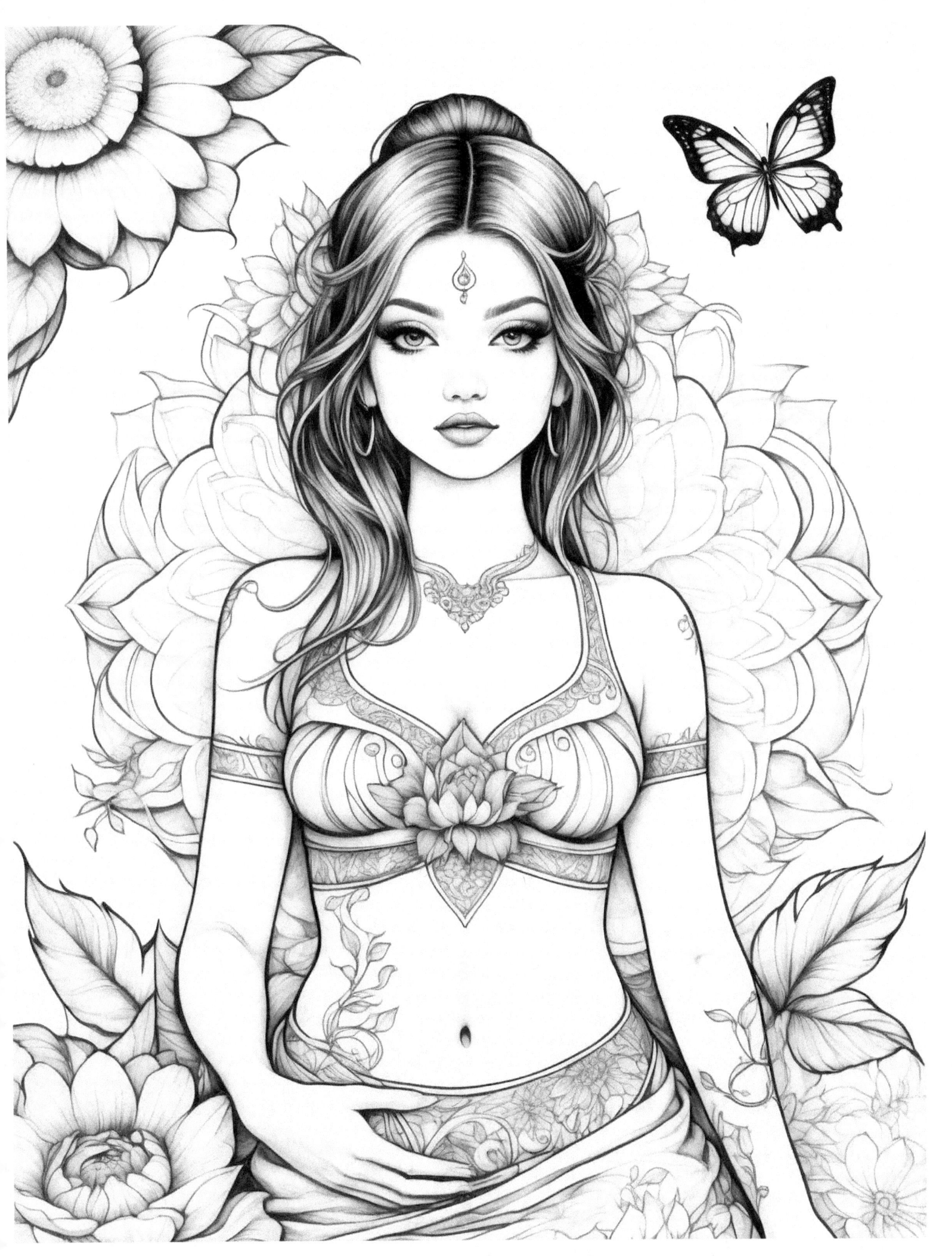

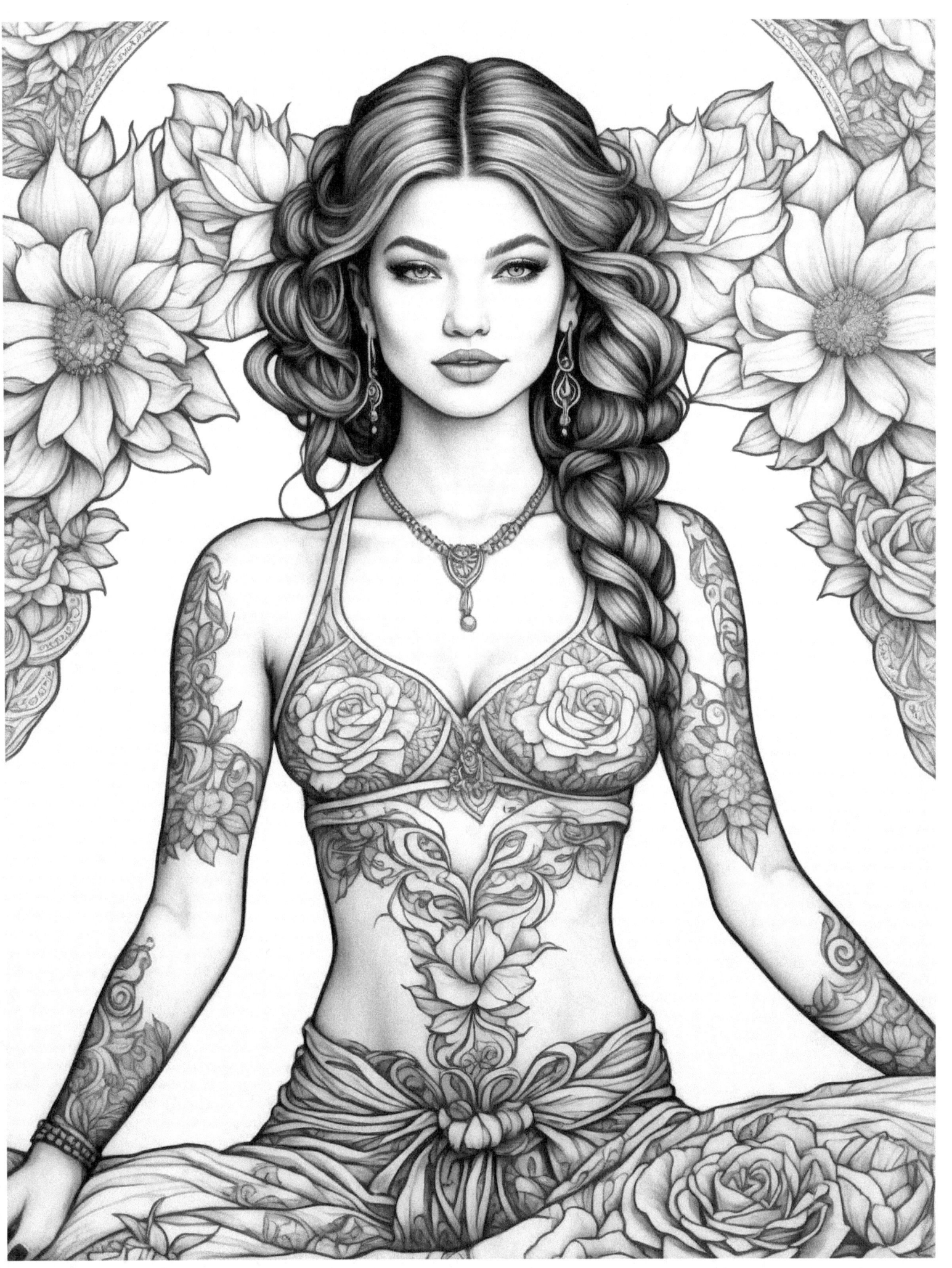

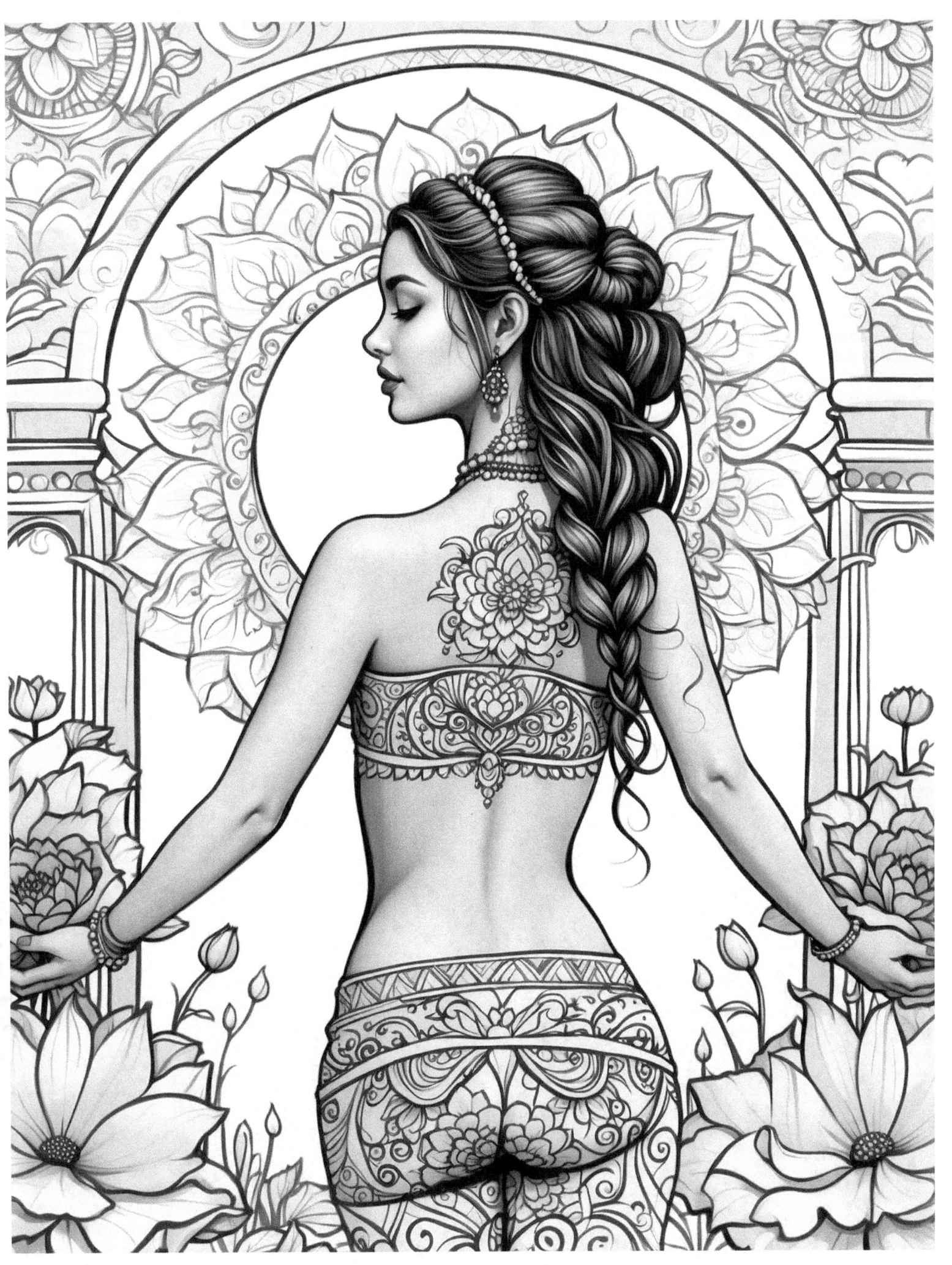

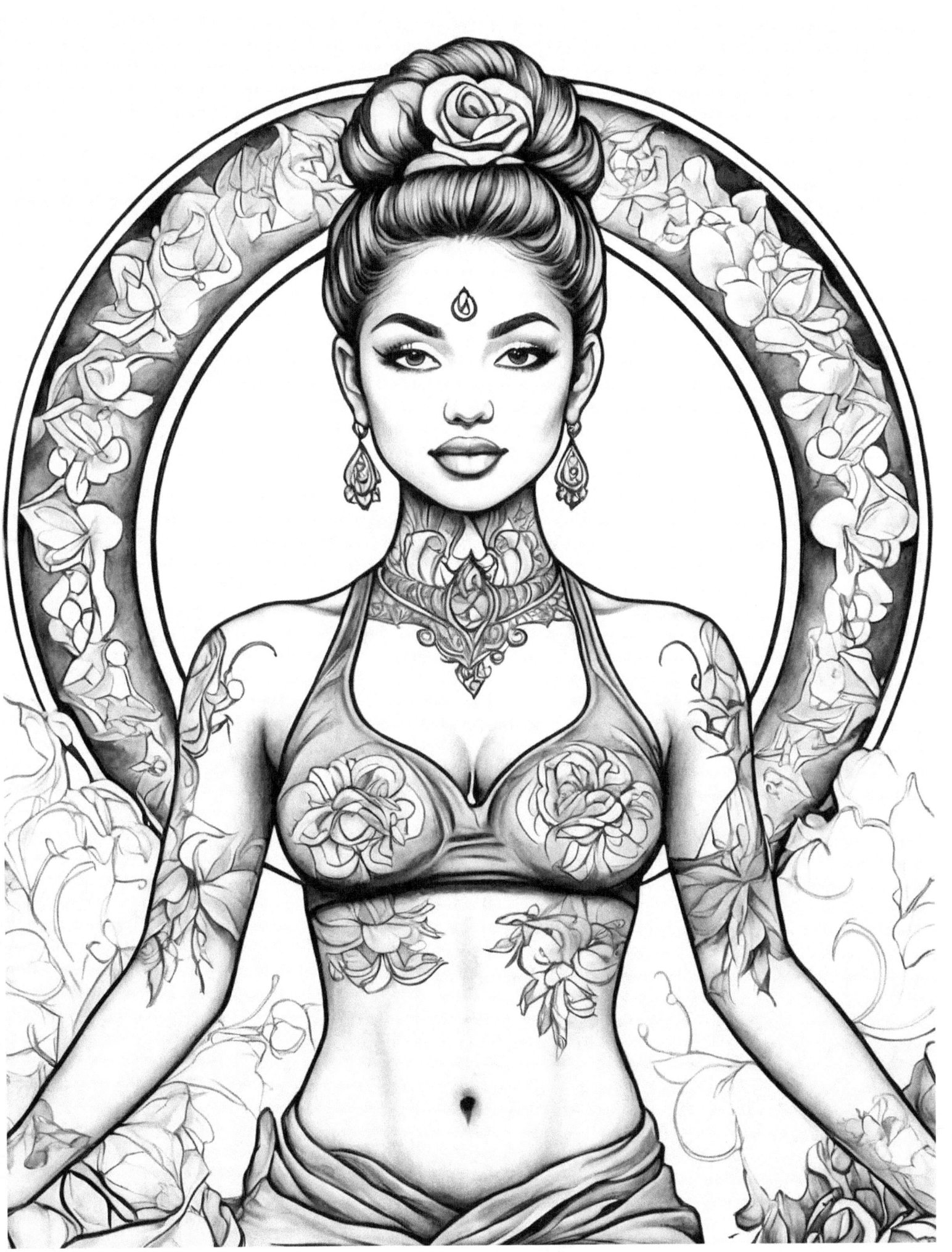

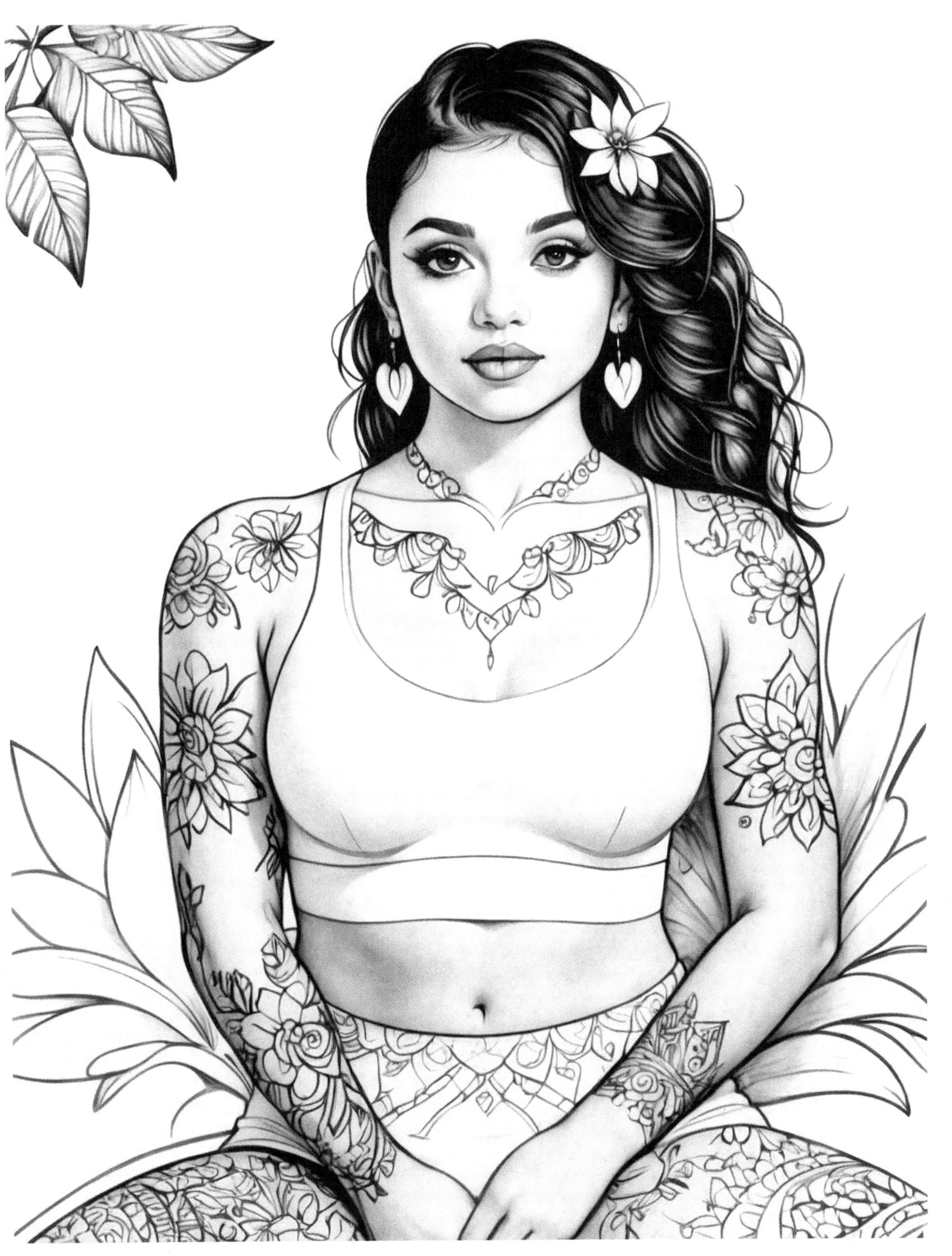

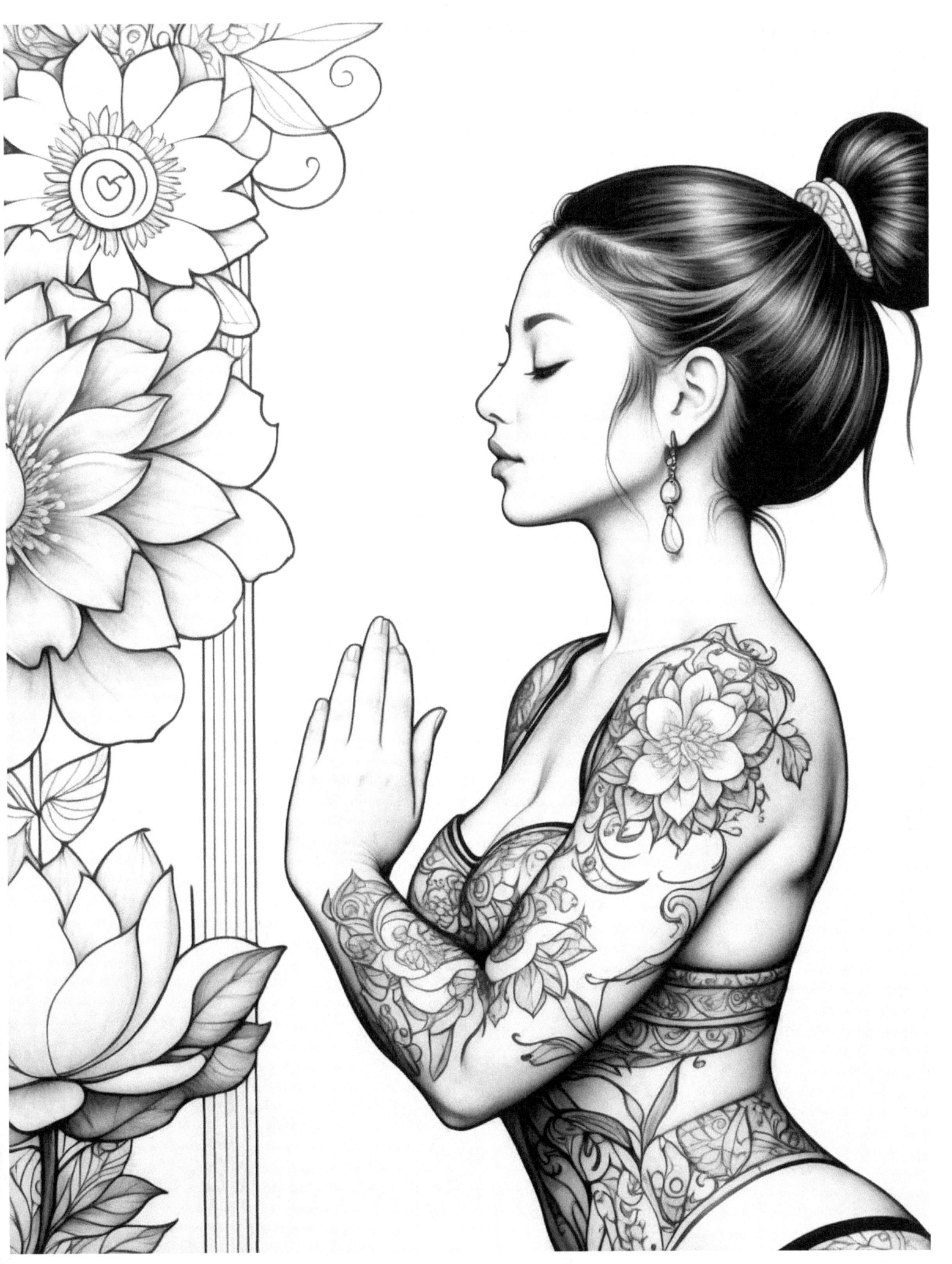

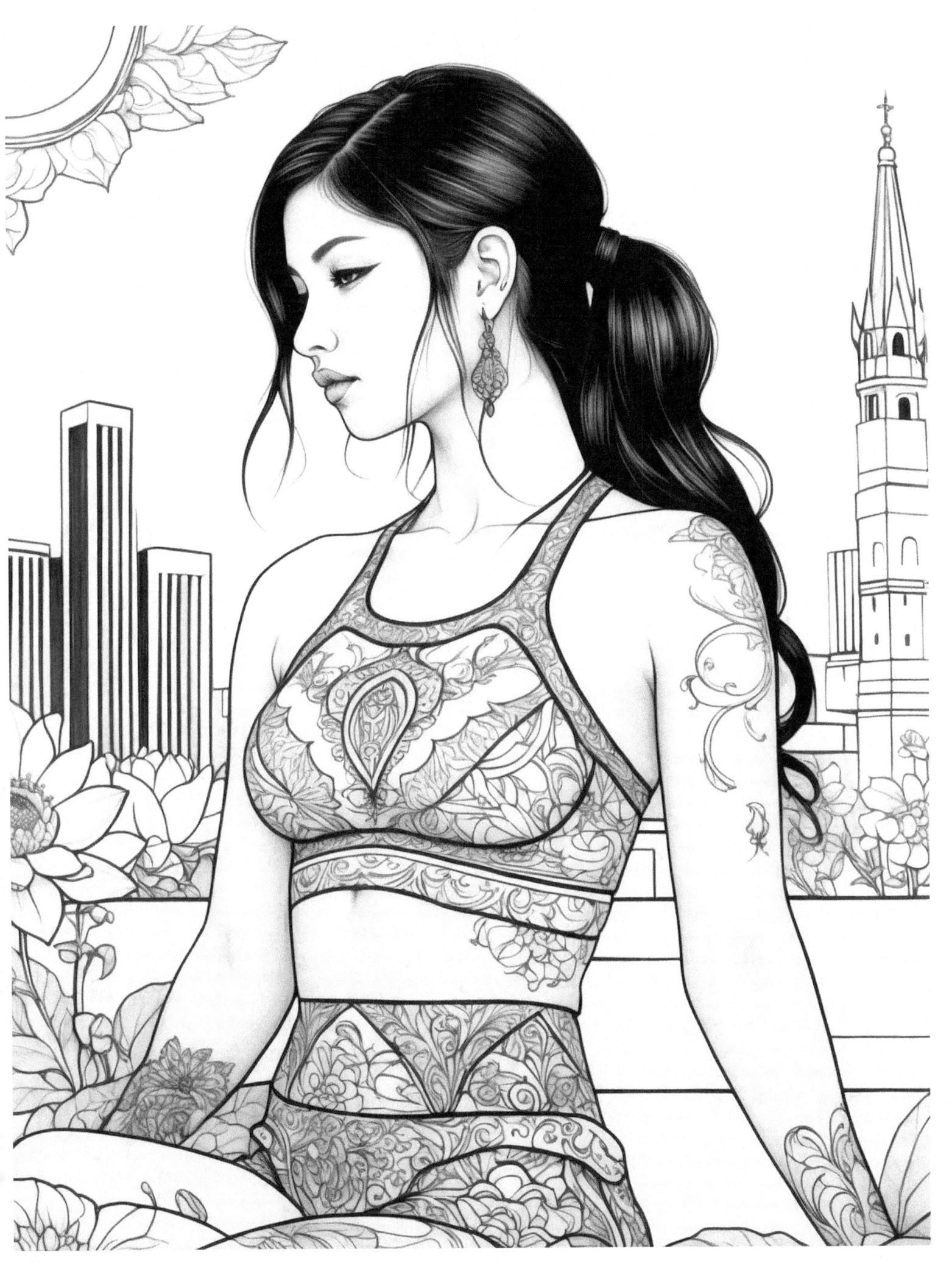

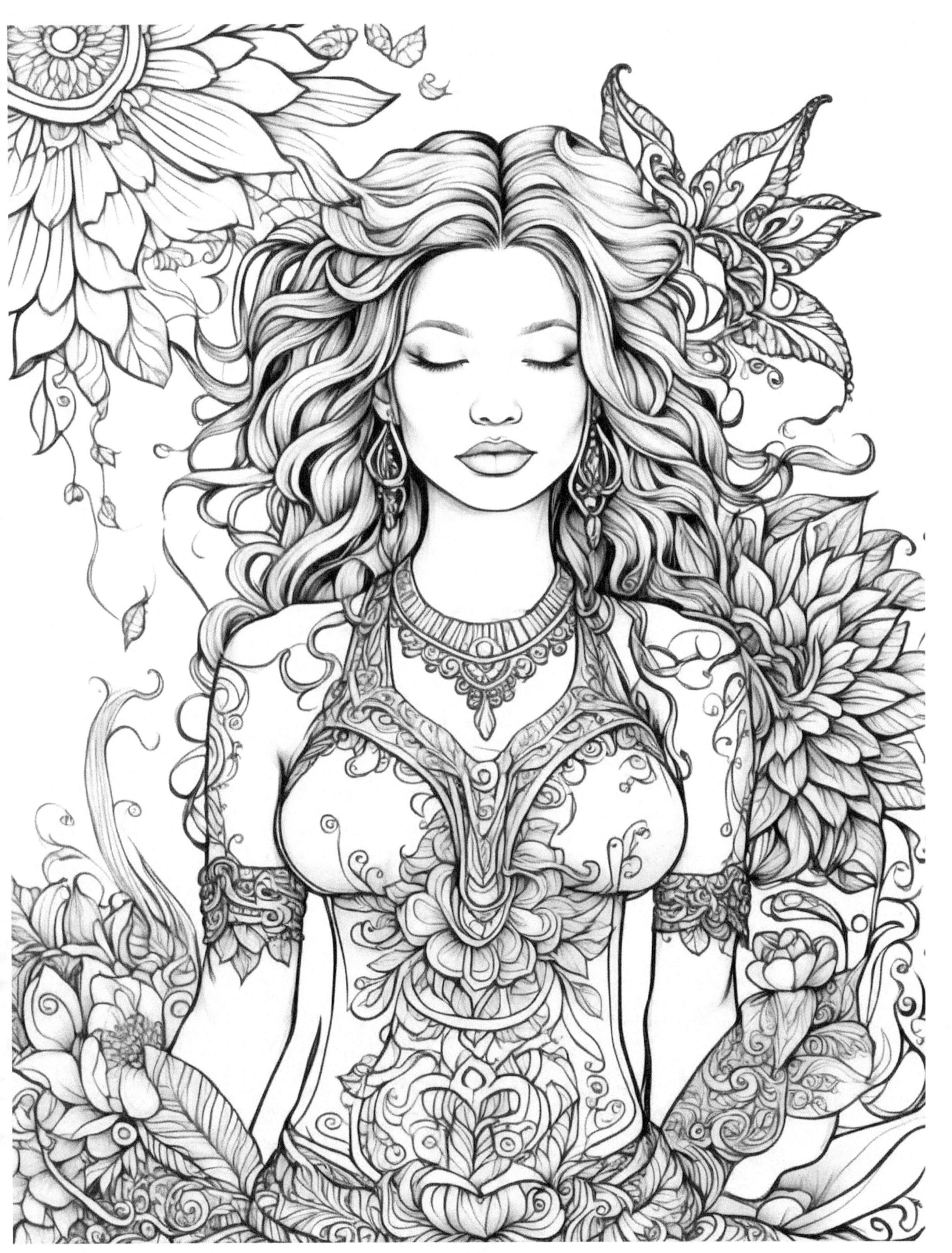

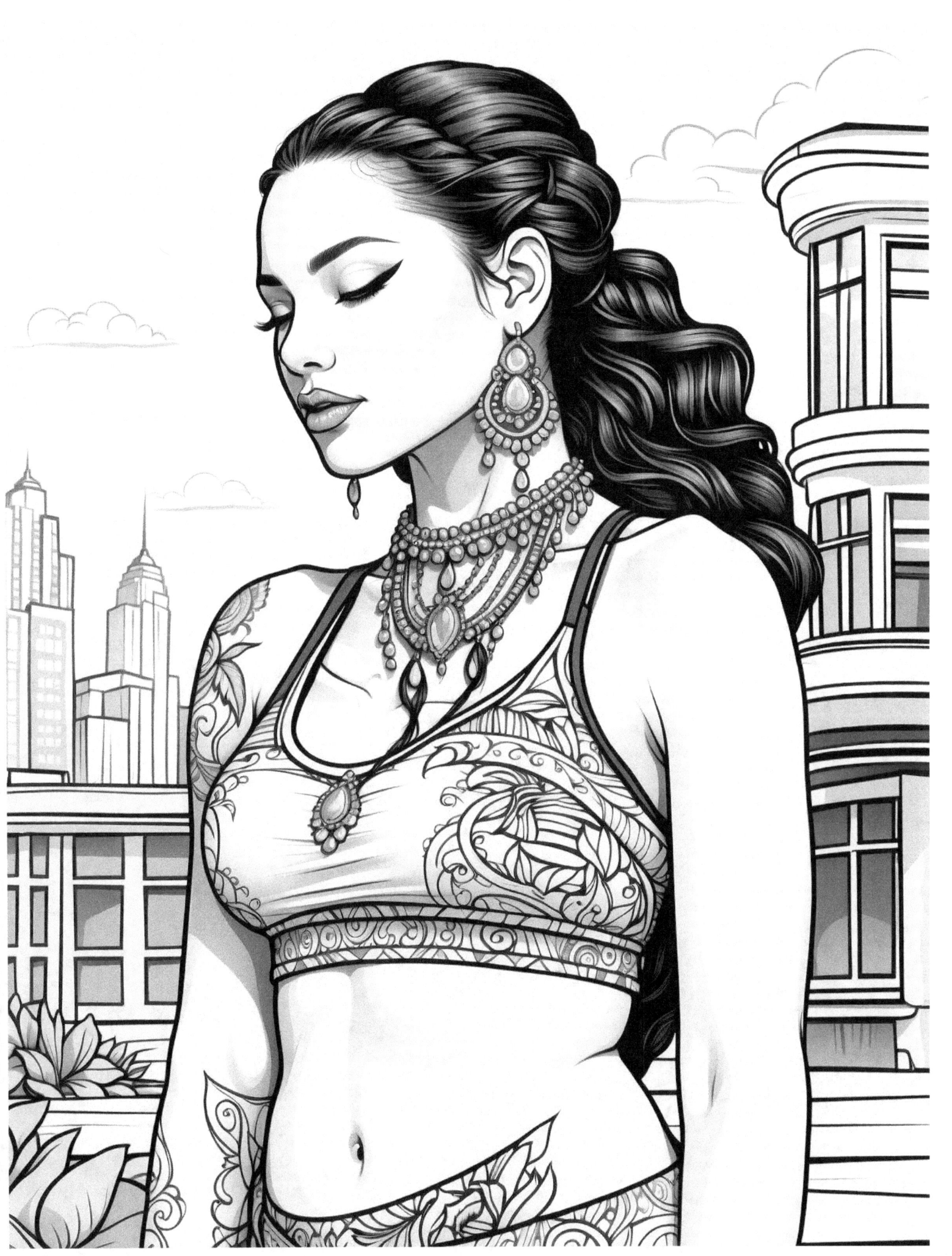

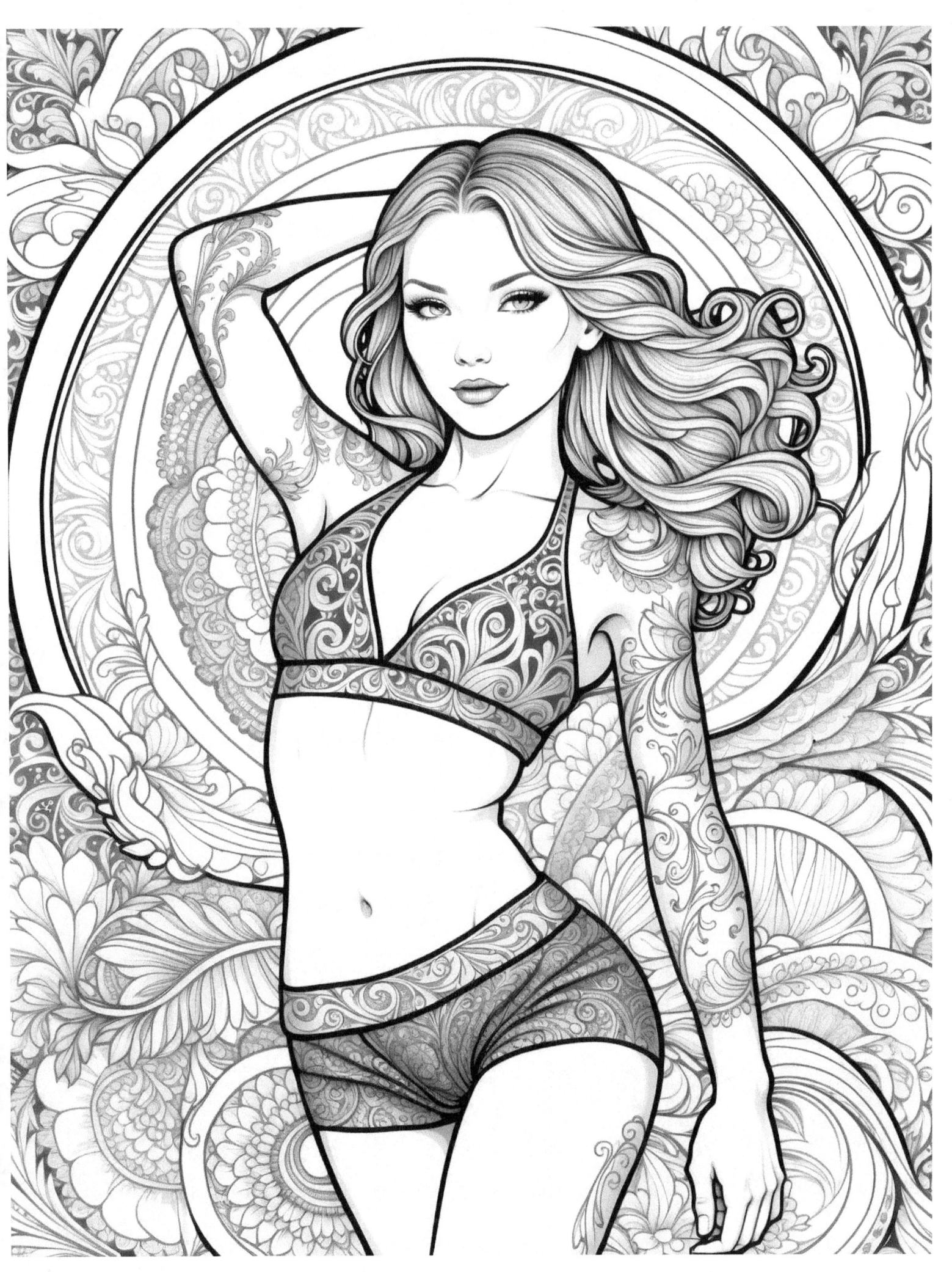

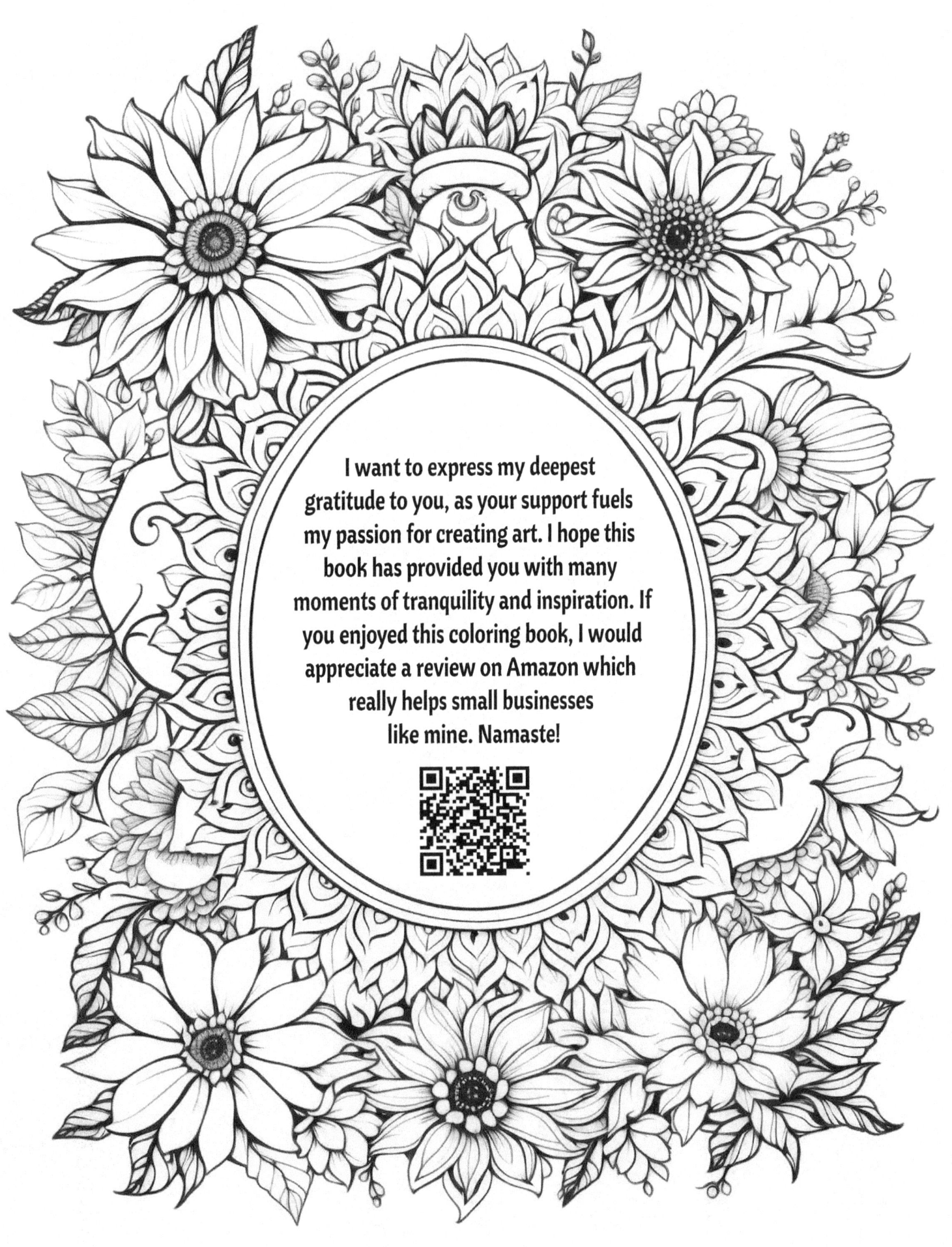

www.ingramcontent.com/pod-product-compliance
Lightning Source LLC
Chambersburg PA
CBHW062118220526
45471CB00010B/3783